Contents **Page**

ON THESE PAGES: Steve McQueen in *The Reivers*, Tony Curtis and Charles Bronson in *The Dubious Patriots*, Stanley Baker and Barbra Streisand at a première, Richard Harris and Alec Guinness in *Cromwell*, Marcello Mastroianni and Sophia Loren in *Sunflower*, Lee Marvin and Jack Palance in *Monte Walsh*, Faye Dunaway in *Puzzle Of A Downfall Child*, Anthony Quinn and Claude Akins in *Nobody Loves Flapping Eagle*

STARS ON THE FRONT AND BACK COVERS

PAUL NEWMAN . SOPHIA LOREN
BARBRA STREISAND . LOUIS ARMSTRONG
RICHARD BURTON . ELIZABETH TAYLOR
RAQUEL WELCH . RICHARD HARRIS
DUSTIN HOFFMAN . STEVE McQUEEN . KIM NOVAK

12/-
(60np)

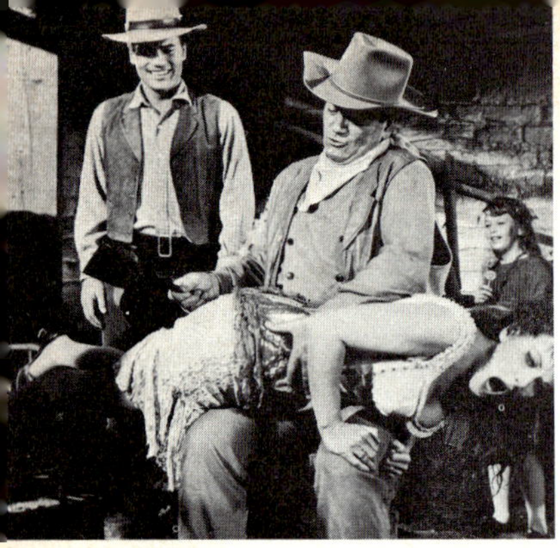

Patrick Wayne with his father, John, in McLintock!

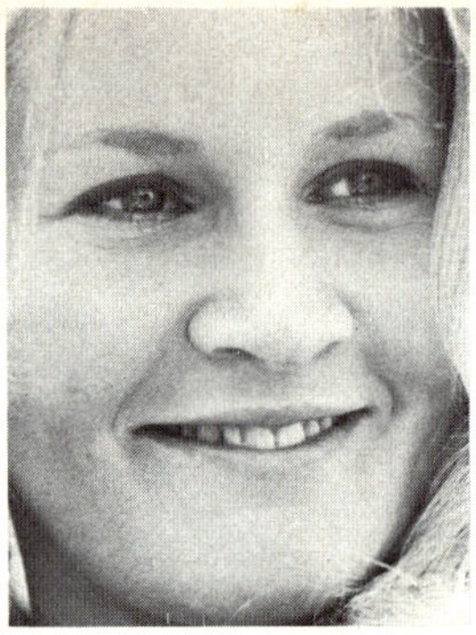

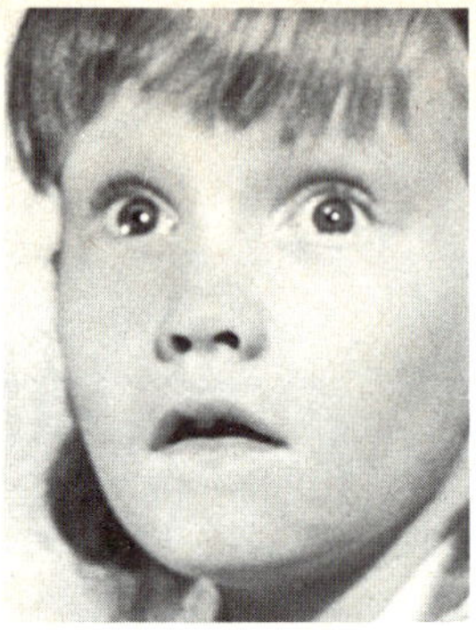

Michele and Karen Dotrice. Michele is seen in And Soon The Darkness. *Karen was in* Mary Poppins

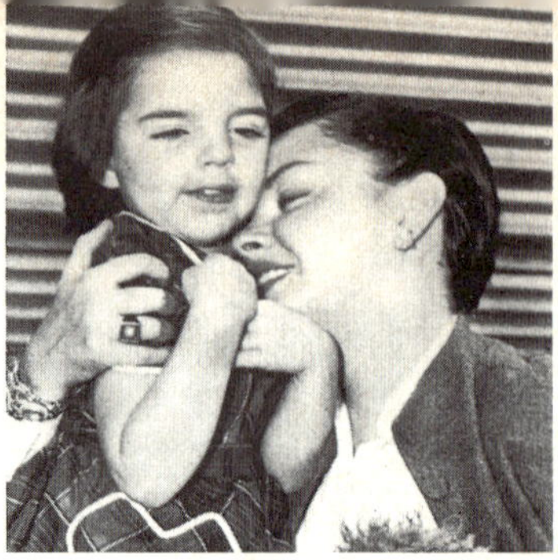

A young Liza Minnelli with her mother, Judy Garland

A talented Mills foursome

Peter Fonda, a big hit in Easy Rider

Henry Fonda and daughter Jane in her earlier acting days

Vanessa Redgrave

Corin Redgrave and his father Michael with Sinead Cusack in David Copperfield

Lynn Redgrave, her mother Rachel Kempson, and Hywel Bennett in The Virgin Soldiers

Geraldine Chaplin with a model of her very famous father, Charles Chaplin

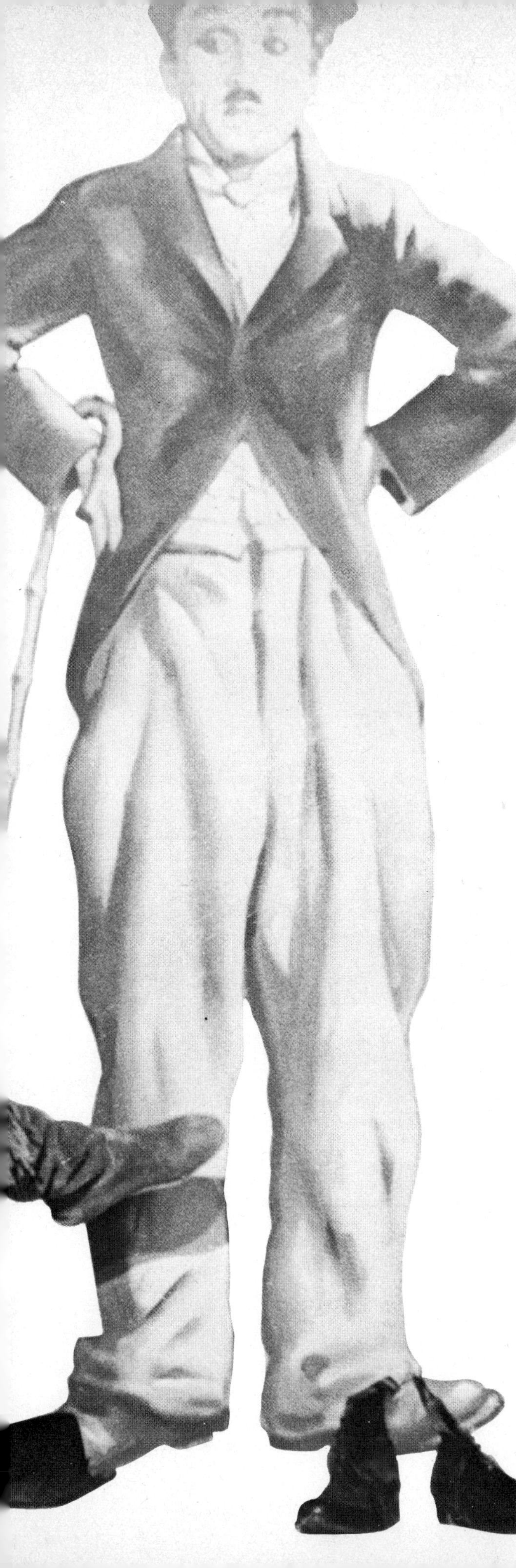

12/-

● Acting runs in families and seems to have done so since time immemorial. As far back as the days of Elizabeth the First there was James Burbage and his even more famous son Richard, who was the star of the Globe Theatre, Southwark, and the plays William Shakespeare was writing for it.

In the late 18th and early 19th centuries, two famous actors, Edmund Kean and Charles Mathews, were both followed successfully on the stage by their sons, each of whom, incidentally, was called Charles. The great Sir Henry Irving of late Victorian days had two acting sons, H. B. and Laurence, whose contemporaries in America were the Drews, a theatrical family who were leading lights of the stage from 1846 to 1927 and whose nephews and niece were John, Lionel and Ethel Barrymore. These three were known (with their father, Maurice Barrymore) as the Royal Family of Broadway and their fame, of course, was repeated in films, there actually being one occasion when all three appeared in the same picture, *Rasputin And The Empress* (1932).

Remember Tyrone Power, who died so prematurely in 1958? His great-grandfather (also named Tyrone Power and born as far back as 1795) was also an actor, and although his grandfather was not attracted to the stage, his own father (again named Tyrone Power) was a famous American actor who appeared in many silent films and early talkies, one of the latter being *The Big Trail* (1931), which, almost incredibly, starred a very young John Wayne. Now Romina and Taryn Power, the late Tyrone's daughters, have started careers in films.

And so the tradition continues. New stars of today are the children of the great stars of yesterday, many of whom, it must be recorded, are still stars today. Some, of course, are no longer with us, as in the case of the unforgettable Judy Garland who, however, has left us a most welcome and delightful legacy in the person of her daughter, Liza Minnelli.

John Garfield, the brilliant actor who died at the early age of thirty-nine, left behind him a son and a daughter who have already made an impression in pictures: John, Jr., who we saw in *That Cold Day In The Park* and Julie, who after two

(continued overleaf)

ACTING! ...it runs in the family

Leslie Wilkinson spotlights those now walking in their parents' footsteps

Michael Douglas with his father, Kirk, proud of his son's ability

Tisa Farrow, sister of Mia, daughter of Maureen O'Sullivan

AND WILL THESE FOLLOW IN DAD'S FOOTSTEPS?

Roger Moore, his wife Luisa, and their two children Deborah and Geoffrey

Anthony Quinn with one of his sons, Lorenzo

(continued)

small roles in *Goodbye, Columbus* and *John And Mary*, was signed for an important part in the latest Jon Voight film, *The Revolutionary*.

Family names which immediately spring to mind are, of course, the Mills, the Redgraves and the Fondas, more especially when one recalls films in which members of the same family have appeared together.

The Family Way (1966) was a most appropriate title for a film which starred both John and Hayley Mills, although they had appeared together in Hayley's first film, *Tiger Bay* (1959) as well as other movies. We still have to see them appearing with John's elder actress daughter, Juliet.

The Redgraves are another big name among film families. Sir Michael's father Roy Redgrave and his mother Margaret Scudamore were both noted stage players . . . and although he has acted several times on stage with his daughter Vanessa, they have never yet starred together in a film, though both played small roles in *Oh, What A Lovely War*. He has, however, appeared in the same film with his son Corin – *David Copperfield* (1969) – in which Sir Michael played Daniel Peggotty and Corin was the handsome Steerforth.

Daughter Lynn, on the other hand, has played in two films with her mother, Lady Redgrave (Rachel Kempson) – *Georgy Girl* (1966) and *The Virgin Soldiers* (1969). And Rachel Kempson played opposite her husband in *The Captive Heart* (1946).

The Fondas – Henry, Jane and Peter – are all scoring in their own highly individual ways – and a family which has a very great name at its head should certainly not be overlooked: the family of Charles Chaplin.

By his marriage to Lita Grey, Charles Chaplin had two sons, Charles, Jr. and Sydney, both of whom appeared in their father's *Limelight* (1952). Charles, Jr. is now dead, but Sydney, although primarily a stage actor (he co-starred with Barbra Streisand in the Broadway production of "Funny Girl") occasionally appears in films and was in his father's production of *A Countess From Hong Kong* (1966).

But Charles Chaplin's later marriage to Oona O'Neill, which produced a family of eight children, has resulted so far in three of these attempting film careers. Up till now, Geraldine has been the most successful (*Doctor Zhivago* 1966). Now we await the film debut of daughter Victoria.

Farrow is another famous film family name. John Farrow, who went to Hollywood from Australia in the mid-1930s, appeared briefly in pictures, but won fame as a writer-director of films. Farrow, who died in 1963, was married to the lovely Maureen O'Sullivan (the original "Jane" to Johnny Weissmuller's "Tarzan"), who had prominent roles in many films. John and Maureen are, of course, the parents of Mia Farrow (of *Rosemary's Baby* and *John And Mary* fame) . . . and now another daughter, Tisa, described as "one of the most exciting new faces to go before the cameras this year", makes her motion picture debut in *Homer*, starring Don Scardino.

Pat Wayne (son of John) and Jim Mitchum (son of Robert) have appeared in films.

Great things are expected of Michael Douglas (son of Kirk), whose success in *Hail, Hero* has been followed by the lead role in *Adam At Six A.M.* Beau Bridges (son of Lloyd) has also made a considerable impression in *Chicago, Chicago*.

Nearer home we have Sinead Cusack, daughter of the famous Irish actor, Cyril Cusack. They appeared together in the recent *David Copperfield* as Little Emily and Barkis respectively. She also starred with Peter Sellers in *Hoffman*.

And now, perhaps someday to rival the Redgraves, we have the Dotrices. Father Roy is a distinguished stage actor, daughter Karen (aged thirteen) has already made three films, including *Mary Poppins*, and now elder sister Michele stars with Pamela Franklin in *And Soon The Darkness*.

Think, too, of famous sisters like Olivia de Havilland and Joan Fontaine and such a talented brother and sister as Warren Beatty and Shirley MacLaine.

The cry of "Nepotism!" can always be raised ("they only got the parts because their father was in the business") . . . but who would dispute that the foregoing would not have reached their present stellar positions even if their parents had not been connected with the world of films?

"I don't want to be surrounded by an atmosphere that encourages me to take myself seriously. Acting is fun for me," says Voight.

by Sally Francis

VOIGHT

THE RELUCTANT STAR!

● It took nine years of solid work in theatre, television and small movie roles for Jon Voight to emerge as a new international "instant success". What did it was his forceful portrayal of the "Midnight Cowboy" Joe Buck, the Texas hustler who tried his luck at selling himself to rich women.

Voight, typically, turned down many super-star roles in lavish productions, following this success, in favour of playing the young student "A", an idealistic though somewhat inept radical, in the modestly budgeted Pressman-Williams production *The Revolutionary*.

Jon Voight is wary about his sudden new fame and its effect on other people. "I don't want to be surrounded by an atmosphere that encourages me to take myself seriously. Acting is fun for me. That part is good and healthy. But right now I'm aware – maybe even over aware – of how even one film success can distort a person's values," he maintains. "I love films, but even more than that I love living, and if films got in the way of that in its fullest sense, I'd give up making films."

After early stage appearances with a Vermont company, Jon spent a year with drama coach Josh Shelley in New York learning Method acting. He later played roles in such TV series as "Gunsmoke" and "Cimarron Strip".

"The television people were very good to me when I was broke and needed to work," he says. "I'd always try to go back for a show if they asked for me."

Jon added to his growing reputation with off-Broadway leads in "A View From The Bridge" with Robert Duvall, and an award-winning performance in "That Summer, That Fall".

When director Paul Williams and producer Ed Pressman first talked to Jon about their film *Out Of It*, they were impressed by his rapid grasp of the character they had in mind for him.

Out Of It, filmed in the summer of 1967, was Jon's first important film role.

From there, he was cast for *Midnight Cowboy*, his big breakthrough, and subsequently for Mike Nichols' *Catch 22* as Milo Minderbender.

The Revolutionary brings him a script which he finds stimulating. His co-star is Jennifer Salt, who also appeared briefly in *Midnight Cowboy*.

"The character is a truthful one, and that's what I hope to make of it," says Voight.

His attitude towards the great rave notices for *Cowboy* that helped make the world aware of the new, big talent, is a careful, watchful one. "Back there in Vermont they said – and rightly at the time – that I couldn't walk or talk. Well, let's say that I can walk and talk now," he says with a grin.

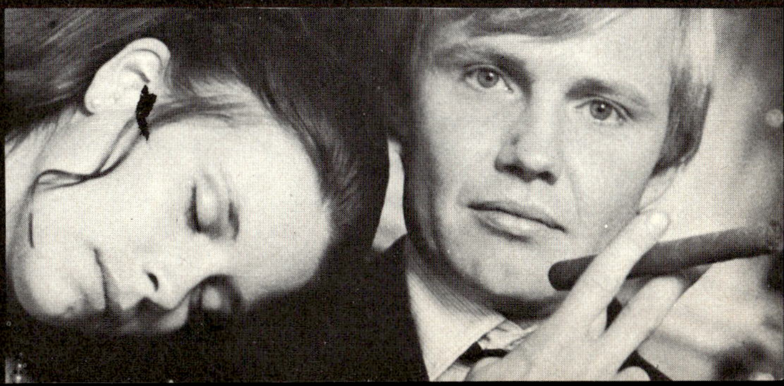

Jon co-stars with Jennifer Salt in The Revolutionary

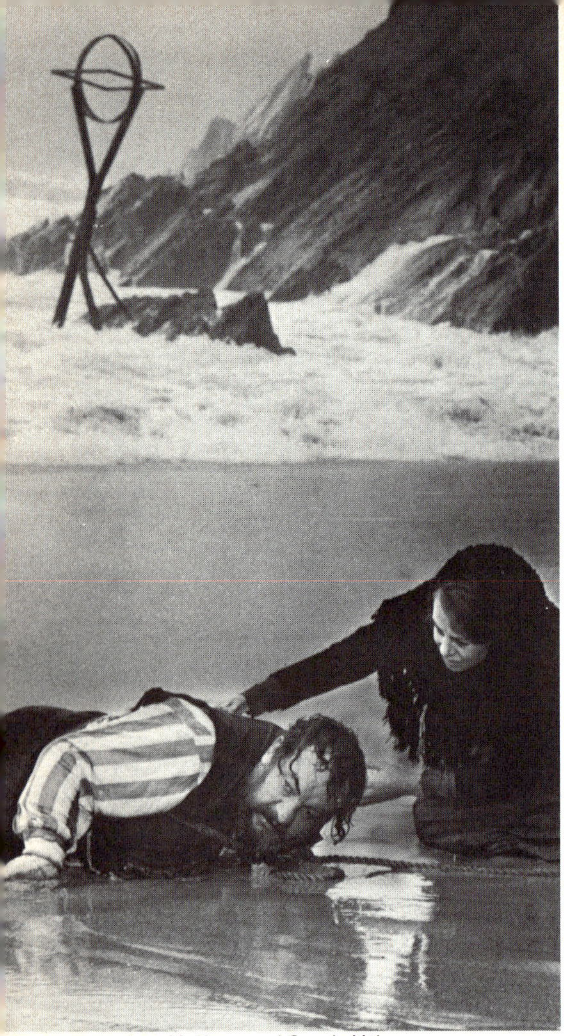

Leo McKern and Sarah Miles

Sarah Miles plays the wife of schoolmaster Mitchum

John Mills as the idiot

Sarah Miles and Christopher Jones

BRIDGE ON THE RIVER KWAI LAWRENCE OF ARABIA

DAVID LEAN'S 'RYAN'S

● A film from the immensely talented director, David Lean, has become a cinematic event. He doesn't make many films, but when he does we have come to expect something of major importance.

Ryan's Daughter is Lean's fourth film in the last fourteen years. The others? Well, there was *The Bridge On The River Kwai.* Then came *Lawrence Of Arabia*, followed by *Doctor Zhivago.* Three superb and highly honoured productions which have earned themselves a prominent place in movie history.

Lean, a shy and modest man who prefers to remain in the background, is a perfectionist in the art of film-making. "Making a film is like a love affair for me," he says. "I fall in love with a subject, and that's that. I just have to film it."

Lean says: "Being a director is a lonely job. You are in the midst of a crowd, but you are on your own. Everyone else looks to you. But to be quite honest with you, I wouldn't know what to do with myself if I wasn't making movies."

As Lean is acclaimed to be one of the leading film story-tellers in the world, so Robert Bolt who wrote the scripts for Lean's *Lawrence Of Arabia*, *Doctor Zhivago*, and for *Ryan's Daughter* (he also wrote the script for *A Man For All Seasons*), is known as the finest screen-writer. Lean and Bolt are a superb team as their past efforts have proved.

Bolt's wife, Sarah Miles, plays the title role in their new film. And as Rosy, daughter of publican Tom Ryan, she marks a change in direction for Lean whose films in recent years have predominantly featured men – Alec Guinness, Peter O'Toole, Omar Sharif.

Rosy more than redresses the balance for in this original, moving story she is the pivot, with five men all more or less in love with her. There's Robert Mitchum as her gentle, shy schoolmaster husband; Christopher Jones, an aristocratic British officer with whom she has a passionate affair; Leo McKern as her doting father who spoils her, calling her "Princess", and there's John Mills as the village idiot who loves her hopelessly from afar. Trevor Howard is the odd man out as Father Collins, a peasant priest, but even *he* has a strong, fatherly affection for the girl.

Sarah Miles, in one of the most important female roles of the year, considers Rosy as "the most wonderful part ever written for a girl". For Sarah, screen acclaim first came as a result of her debut film *Term Of Trial* in which she starred with Laurence Olivier,

A movie village is built

The village seen in the film

Trevor Howard plays a priest

which was followed by *The Servant*.

She met Robert Bolt soon after making a very brief appearance in *Blow-Up*, and for a time virtually gave up her acting career. Said Sarah: "I learned more about acting by not acting than I had ever learned before. It gave me the chance to stand back and take stock, to realise my mistakes. If you are immersed in the business constantly you do not have this opportunity. I used to think sincerity was enough and cared nothing for technique. I know now that by using technique you can give a more sincere performance. I am happier with my work in *Ryan's Daughter* than with anything I have ever done."

Ryan's Daughter is essentially a story about people – a poor, isolated community in the far west of Ireland in 1916 who are governed by a strict moral code, which if broken, means hell for the transgressor.

These villagers of Kirrary with their sufferings, their joys, their dreams and their sorrows, their doubts and their fears will be easily recognised by us all.

We first see Rosy as a fascinating girl who ends up as a considerable woman. Robert Bolt says: "Her story is about the universal attempt of youth to get something for nothing . . . and the realisation that something has to be paid for anything. Which makes an adult of an adolescent. I hope we have a truthful story of high emotion, one in which sex is seen as the trigger, in proper balance with trust and tenderness, which are as necessary to love as courage and passion."

Leo McKern describes his role of Rosy's father as "a pathetic windbag of a creature". He is the rich man of the village who wants to be all things to all men, an uncertain patriot whose loyalties are divided between his fellow countrymen and the hated British garrison down the road.

In other top roles Robert Mitchum, playing one of the most unusual roles of his career, may well be on his way to an Oscar if advance reports are anything to go by. His performance as the village schoolmaster might surely rate as the finest he's ever given. Trevor Howard plays a priest for the first time on the screen, and the exciting young Christopher Jones (*Wild In The Streets* and *The Looking Glass War*) portrays the war-shattered British officer. John Mills portrays his most unusual screen role.

A special village was constructed for this large-scale production, and like the film's stars showed distinct signs of wear at the end of the long and arduous months of filming.

But in *Ryan's Daughter* we could be hailing another great screen classic.

DOCTOR ZHIVAGO and now . . .

DAUGHTER'

According to director David Lean, film-making is a lonely business. A film by this excellent director is usually a big event.

William Holden's boyish looks were first seen on the screen in 1939 with a starring role in *Golden Boy*

Natalie Wood played many girlish roles before she became the mature star of today

James Stewart hasn't changed all that much. He was always lean faced. He's been in films for 35 years

A young Burton sets out on his way to becoming one of our great actors. He made his film debut in 1948

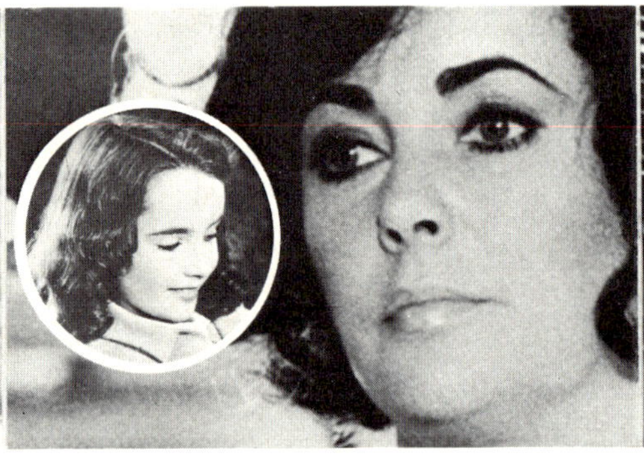

Liz Taylor has always been gorgeous to look at, and to think this was how we first saw her in movies

Kirk Douglas always did have that rugged look which was to win him many rough, mean guy parts

Sophia Loren is far more sophisticated and beautiful today than she was when starting out on the road to fame

Stanley Baker looks at himself as he appeared in an early film, *Beautiful Stranger*

Julie Andrews started her showbiz career at an early age little dreaming how big a star she was destined to be

"I wasn't a bad looking guy was I?" asks Henry Fonda. He wasn't, as this early picture shows

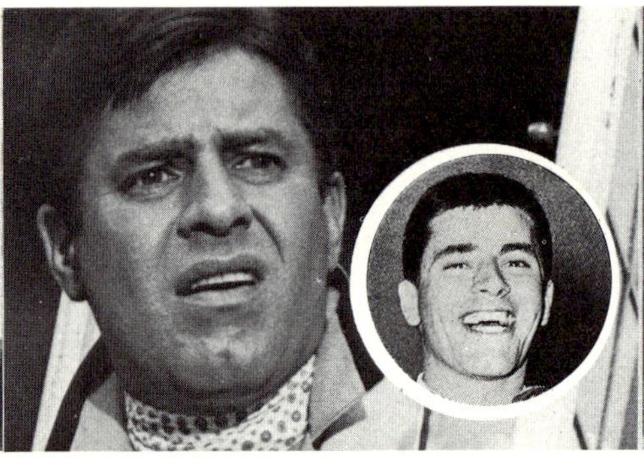

Jerry Lewis back in the days when he first teamed up with former partner Dean Martin

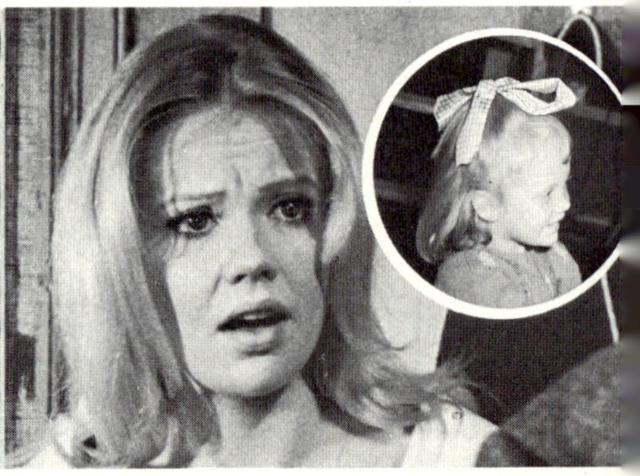

Hayley Mills at the age of five. She's grown into a lovely and talented young woman with great acting abilities

It's Dirk Bogarde back in 1947 in the film *Esther Waters*. Dirk is still one of our top actors

Barbara Stanwyck gazes back over thirty years to when she was seen in *Golden Boy* in 1939

For Rock Hudson, acting was a dream till after his early Navy days. In those days his name was Roy Fitzgerald

Bette Davis was a classic beauty in her youth. She is still a fascinating-looking woman and a great actress

Yep, John Wayne's ridden many a trail since he first rode his way into moviegoers' hearts

"Now why show me like that," Sinatra might be saying at the sight of a young, skinny Sinatra

Tony Curtis really was a beautiful baby. Ahead of him was great international screen success

Richard Attenborough was to find himself haunted by his youngish looks later in his career

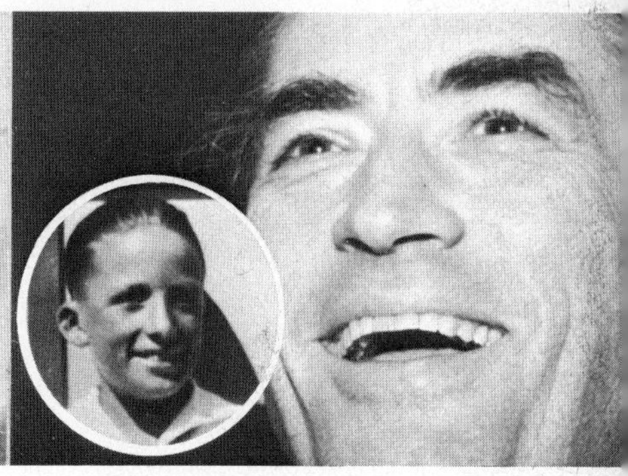

Gregory Peck in the days when fame and fortune were still a long way off. Greg still looks great

OUCH! WAS THAT REALLY ME!

THE THREE FACES OF Fear

CHRISTOPHER LEE
VINCENT PRICE
PETER CUSHING

● Horror is at best a nebulous entity. No one really knows what frightens another person. While one man is scared of the dark, another might become hysterical if confronted by a snake. In George Orwell's famous book "1984", the most dreaded torture was to be placed in a room where special equipment delved into the prisoner's subconscious, finding out his own special terror and then subjecting him to it.

We are still a long way from machines able to achieve that, but there are three men in the movie business who have got a pretty shrewd idea about what frightens most people. The men are Vincent Price, Christopher Lee and Peter Cushing. Each has a different sphere in which to operate his own brand of fear with which to terrify the public.

Lee is a master at playing horror roles. During his long career he has played such varied parts as Frankenstein's monster, the inscrutable Chinese master-mind Dr. Fu Manchu, and Rasputin, the mad Russian monk who surrounded himself with evil. But perhaps his most successful part, the one in which he has terrified the most people, is that of the undead vampire, Count Dracula. For this role he wears a wig, pasty make-up, false fangs and red contact lenses.

Christopher's attitude to the role is that "one must immerse oneself completely in the character and forget one's own personality entirely. The portrayal from start to finish must be straight, honest and sincere."

Though Lee is adamant that Dracula must only be looked upon as just one of his many and varied roles, there is little doubt that when people have nightmares which feature creatures from beyond the grave, the terror that confronts them always looks a little like Christopher Lee as Dracula, fangs and all. There can be no higher praise for acting ability than that.

Vincent Price looks equally as terrifying as Lee. But where Lee's eyes are deep-set and foreboding, Price's are sparkling, surrounded by bushy eyebrows. He smiles often, and has a kind, almost gentle way of speaking.

Possibly this is why he has made his mark not as a ghoul, but as a series of men scorned by the rest of humanity, usually because of physical deformity or insanity, who take out their frustrations on screaming victims.

Price is a Yale graduate, he is also a respected art critic, an expert on Red Indian folk-lore and an exceptional cook, and he has written a very successful cookery book.

In his long film career, he has played almost every type of part imaginable. He's somewhat a comedian with a keen sense of humour. A far cry from the evil Matthew Hopkins in *Witchfinder General*, or the succession of lunatics from the classic novels of Edgar Allan Poe.

He is a little cynical about the public's appetite for horror. "The public's eager acceptance of horror films is because they see them only as make-believe, an escape into fantasy." He says he doesn't really think horror films are horrible. "They are just another form of fairy tale. In France, all my horror films play in art theatres, and are written about in *avant-garde* magazines."

Peter Cushing, thin and angular, looks anything but terrifying. His formula is to act as the dedicated man gone astray, so deeply involved with his experiments (he is usually a scientist, often Dr. Frankenstein) that he is willing to break the law, and endanger the lives of his fellows to complete his work.

"People love watching horror films," he told me, "and squirming in their seats, because they know the meaning of real terror, and they see in my type of picture something they know cannot happen, but they can still recoil from it.

"They get a big kick from their own imaginations. They enjoy the experience of having their spines chilled, so they can laugh about it later."

Peter, too, is quiet, gentle and respected by everyone he meets. He likes a quiet life, and spends much of his time at home in Whitstable, enjoying his life away from acting.

So there we are. Three men who are completely unlike their on-screen images who will continue to shock the living daylights out of us all for a long time to come.

LEFT: Christopher Lee in his famous Dracula *role*

BELOW LEFT: Vincent Price "scarred" for The Oblong Box

BELOW: Peter Cushing as he appears in The Vampire Lovers

GREG DAVIS

DUSTIN HOFF

Here is the story behind Dustin Hoffman's graduation from unknown actor to international star

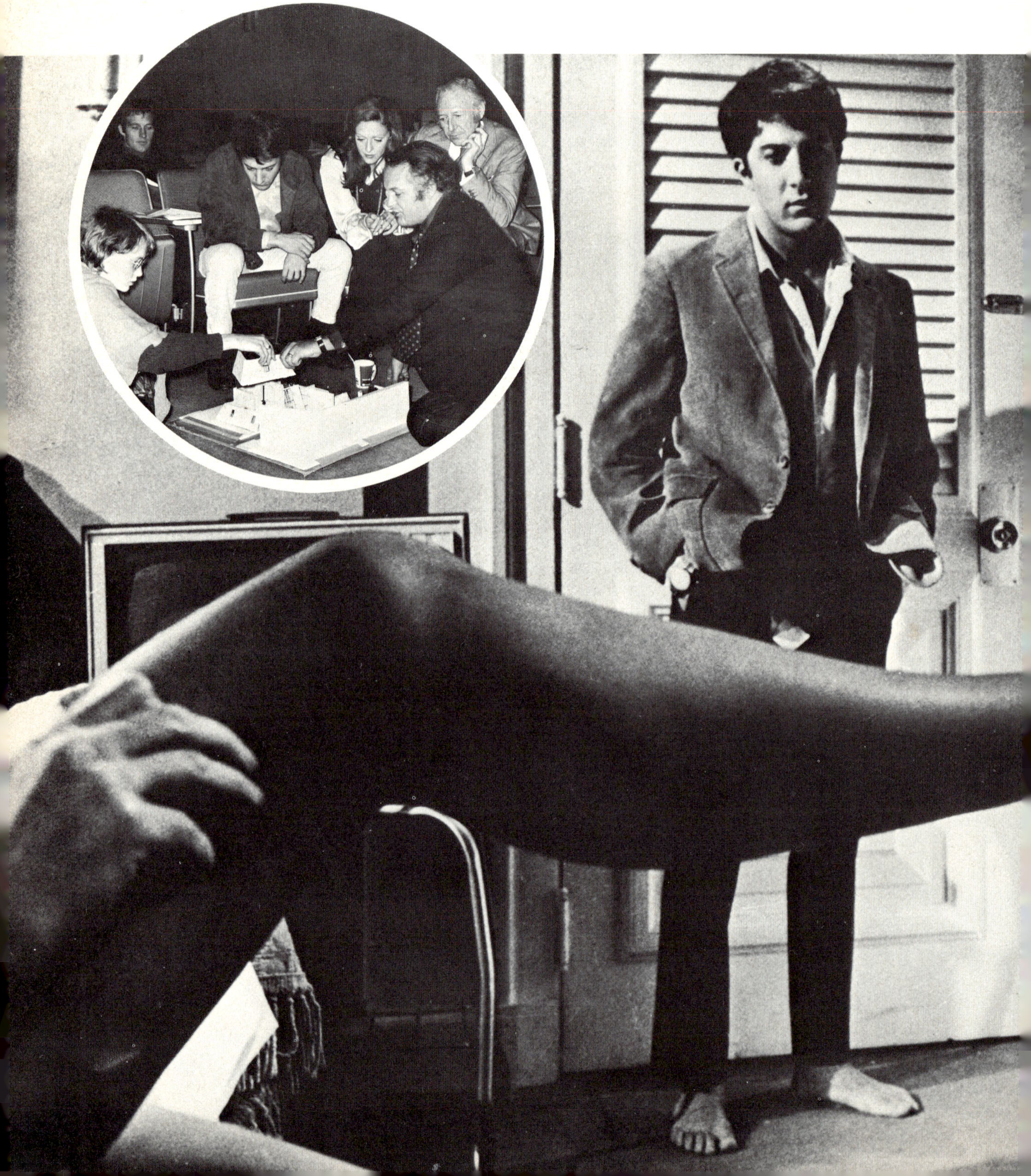

MAN

told by Leslie Wilkinson

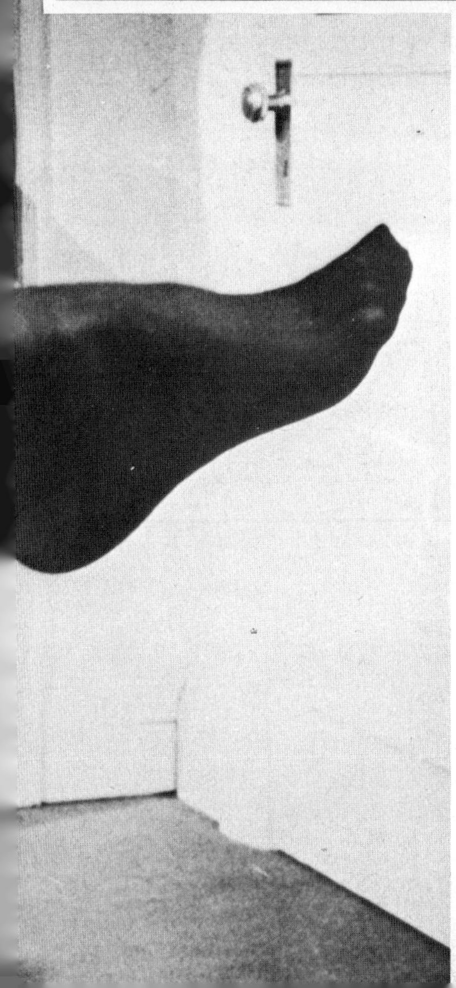

CIRCLE
Dustin and Mia Farrow with director Peter Yates on the set of John And Mary

LEFT
The film that made Dustin a star – The Graduate

ABOVE
Dustin and Faye Dunaway together in Little Big Man

TOP RIGHT
Midnight Cowboy *won awards for Dustin and Jon Voight*

● We saw him first in *The Graduate*, a brilliant young man covered in college honours, but who nevertheless was a complete ignoramus as far as sex was concerned. But Mrs. Robinson soon helped him to a degree in that subject . . . and the memory of that wide-eyed, confused, almost inarticulate youth of seventeen stayed with us long after we had left the cinema.

Then we saw him again . . . in *Midnight Cowboy* . . . as Ratso, the crippled little con-man, one of the thousands of New York drop-outs, living by his wits, sleeping rough and dreaming hazily of a life that must forever be beyond his reach. So in depth was the character played that we could almost smell him.

And then we came to *John And Mary* and met John, a charming, house-proud, moderately self-sufficient thirtyish young man who feels, however, that he needs a girl and in consequence frequents the "singles" bars with that object in view.

And all this splendid variety is only Dustin Hoffman so far. He should have been discovered by Hollywood long ago . . . but he wasn't. Still, he has started at the top and is definitely destined to stay there.

He was born in Los Angeles on 8th August 1937, a local boy so far as Hollywood was concerned . . . but they apparently didn't want to know him. He had majored in music at Santa Monica City College and had studied at the Los Angeles Conservatory of Music, intending first to become a classical and then a jazz pianist. Thus he was able to do his own piano-playing in *John And Mary*.

But music had to give way to acting and he enrolled at the Pasadena Community Playhouse.

After graduating, he went to New York . . . but the breaks came slowly and at long, long intervals. He admits his parents sent him money, but despite this he had to take a series of jobs to stave off starvation: attendant at a psychiatric institute, a waiter, coat-checker and soft-drink dispenser, toy demonstrator and drama coach at an East Harlem boys' club.

He remembers New York as "cold and lonely and terrifying", but he remained there to land a one-word walk-on in a play called "A Cook for Mr. General", played a one-night stand in "Waiting for Godot", following this with the role of a hunchbacked Nazi homosexual in "Harry, Noon and Night", which led to his being given the lead (as an eccentric Russian clerk) in an off-Broadway production, "Journey of the Fifth Horse".

This won him the Obie (off-Broadway) award as best actor of the year. He then played the cockney plumber in Henry

(continued overleaf)

(continued)
Livings' "Eh?". More awards followed, the London "Times" hailed him as "the finest new American actor" . . . and director Mike Nichols summoned him to Hollywood to test for *The Graduate*.

He did another off-Broadway play – "Jimmy Shine" – between *Midnight Cowboy* and *John And Mary*.

And now his fourth film role is Cinema Center's *Little Big Man*, a most appropriate nickname for Dustin Hoffman himself, for although his height is a mere five feet six and a half inches, his stature, star-appeal-wise, already ranks with that of the six-foot-plus idols of the screen.

Little Big Man himself is Jack Crabb who, still alive at the age of 121, is the sole survivor of Custer's Last Stand in 1876 . . . and we follow him as he recalls his past life: first as a boy of sixteen travelling westward with his parents, who are killed in a raid by the Cheyenne Indians; as a frontiersman; as a "white" Indian during his life with the Cheyenne; as a medicine-show trickster and gunslinger; as a bearded trapper and drunken layabout, and as one of Custer's men at the fatal battle of the Little Big Horn!

The somewhat unusual name of Dustin ("the other kids used to call me 'Dustbin'") was given him by his mother, who had long admired Dustin Farnum, romantic hero of the silent screen.

He's been coined an "anti-star", for Dustin Hoffman has no interest in the status symbols and general ballyhoo which go, or are expected to go, with stardom. He is satisfied that he can now pick and choose his own parts. That is what stardom means to him. The star caste system ("so thick in Hollywood that you can cut it") he loathes.

He is married (since 3rd May 1969) to Anne Byrne, a former ballet dancer, who at the same time brought him a three-year-old stepdaughter. He is a great reader. He listens to music (naturally) and sometimes plays tennis. He is interested in politics, he enjoys being with friends and he has a genuine wit.

Above all, he is a dedicated actor, described by one critic as "miraculous" and "gifted", as another said, "with awesome versatility."

ABOVE
In Little Big Man *Dustin plays the sole survivor of Custer's Last Stand*

BELOW
Bath time for Dustin with Faye Dunaway obliging with some help in Little Big Man

RIGHT
Dustin was superb in the excellent film, Midnight Cowboy, *with the equally brilliant Jon Voight*

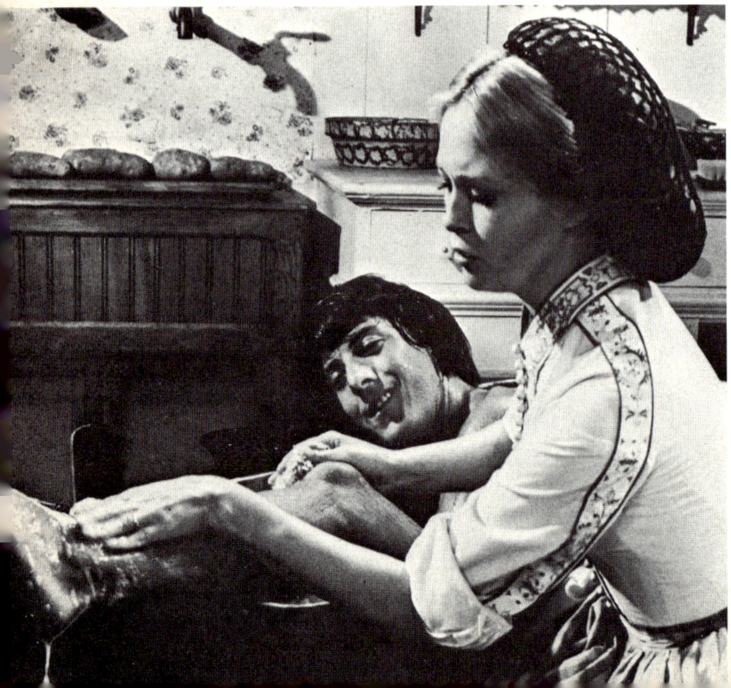

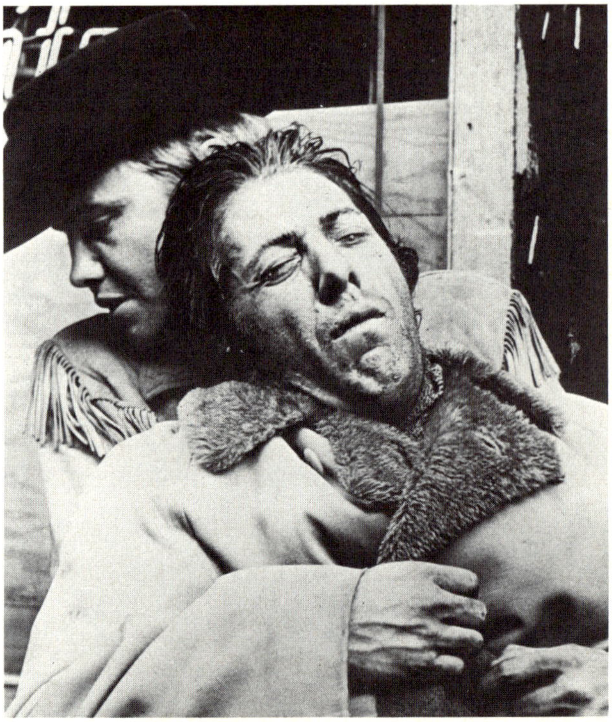

DUSTIN HOFFMAN

12
8

● This fascinating and unusual film authentically re-creates the Olympic Games in order to tell the personal and emotional story of the men who take part in, what many describe as, the most dramatic event of the Games – the Marathon.

The film takes a revealing and compassionate look at a group of runners who compete in the gruelling and torturous twenty-six-mile race. It portrays their tensions and conflicts in the colourful, turbulent and fiercely competitive world in which they live. It follows their progress through the year or so of their lives that leads up to the climactical event as the Marathon is run through the streets of Rome.

The men among the participants are Harry Hayes, a young Englishman trained by an ex-Olympic star, a bitter Olympic Silver Medallist named Bill Oliver; Scott Reynolds, the all-American boy who doesn't know what it means to lose; Sunny Pintubi, an Aborigine managed by two opportunistic Australian bookmakers; and Pavel Vendek, a former Gold Medal Olympic star recruited by the Czechoslovakian government to run the gruelling race again.

The film's director Michael Winner describes his film as being "about people seeking to set themselves above their environment through this unusual physical skill. The use of real countries as backgrounds to their separate achievements is essential."

Location shooting was conducted in several countries around the world including Australia and Japan. For the stirring, breathtaking finale of the Marathon itself, Winner used extensive locations in Rome for the setting of the race, obtaining permission to film in the streets and squares which were closed down for the cameras. These locations included some of the most famous places in the Eternal City – the Colosseum, the Constantine Arch, the Forum, Piazzi di Trevi, Piazza Navona and many others.

To enact the leading characters a number of international stars were signed. Michael Crawford plays Harry Hayes, the naive English milkman who becomes a record-breaking

(continued overleaf)

Charles Aznavour (right) portrays a famous runner who is one of the film's principal characters

OPPOSITE PAGE

TOP LEFT: Michael Crawford represents England

TOP RIGHT: Ryan O'Neal portrays the all-American boy

BELOW: The runners prepare for a spectacular event

THE GAMES

Ken Johns reports on the background behind the filming of a story about the Marathon event in the Olympic Games

THE GAMES *(continued)*

runner under the almost fanatical coaching of Bill Oliver, played by Stanley Baker. Oliver, a frustrated and complex man tries to make his young protégé "run through pain to the top of the world" to compensate for the disappointments of his own life.

The American actor Ryan O'Neal, popular with millions of television viewers as Rodney Harrington in "Peyton Place" enacts the role of Scott Reynolds, the brash and arrogant Yale student.

Pavel Vendek, the Czech "Iron Man" is played by Charles Aznavour internationally known as a singer but now making a valuable contribution to films as a dramatic actor. He has also been seen in *Candy* and *The Adventurers.*

Sunny Pintubi, the Aborigine trained and exploited by two crafty Australian bookmakers is portrayed by twenty-year-old Athol Compton, an Aborigine who has never acted before. Michael Winner was so confident in his abilities to play the role he felt Athol was so right for that he signed him without even a screen test.

Jeremy Kemp is cast as a conniving Australian, Jim Harcourt, whose schemes for Sunny pay off in a big way.

Rafer Johnson, who won a Gold Medal in the Decathlon in the 1960 Olympics in Rome appears in the film as himself, an American television network commentator who announces the events of the Games as they are televised throughout the world.

Other important roles are played by Elaine Taylor (as the young girl friend of Michael Crawford), June Jago, Mona Washbourne, Reg Lye and others.

Before the production went before the cameras, over a year was spent in preparatory work. Michael Winner screened hundreds of hours of film and newsreel footage of previous Olympic Games and also examined official photographs and material connected with Olympic history. He also secured the support of athletic associations and sports committees in all the countries he worked while making the picture.

The famous long-distance runner, Gordon Pirie, was appointed the film's technical adviser and in this capacity he trained and worked out with Michael Crawford as well as supervising many of the athletic details. The other actors who appear as runners were also trained under professional supervision.

Dominating the huge and lavish production was its director Michael Winner. *The Games* is by far the most important and the most expensive film of his career. "The book by Hugh Atkinson was a mammoth novel. The film will be the same – mammoth!" he predicted confidently when I met him on a location in Windsor during the first week of production. "It's going to be quite enormous and I'm going to love making every minute of it."

This exciting film takes a close look into the lives of

ABOVE
Director Michael Winner, Michael Crawford and also Gordon Pirie

LEFT
Michael Crawford, covers the gruelling mile after mile

RIGHT
Stanley Baker plays a bitter ex-athlete, Bill Oliver

Winner is a man who rises to a challenge. He's a man who always gets his own way. He's got to the top of his business, which is making first-rate movies, by sheer persistence and perseverance. "It's not easy to become a success in this business," he says. "You've got to be ready and willing to fight your way up. It's a tough profession." But needless to say he loves every minute of it. "I've always wanted to make films – there was nothing else I wanted to do."

He started off modestly by writing a syndicated film column at fourteen, then he was a call-boy at the BBC-TV studios, then an agent, an assistant director and an editor. He wrote articles for film magazines then started to write, direct and edit short films. His first main feature was a teen musical, *Play It Cool* with Billy Fury, followed by an updated *The Cool Mikado*. *West 11* and *The System* followed, with the latter film gaining him much attention. His first big hit was *You Must Be Joking* an all-star comedy which led next to *The Jokers*, a hit comedy about two young men who steal the Crown Jewels. By now he was firmly established as a film-maker of importance. In 1967 came another dramatic success, *I'll Never Forget What's 'Is Name* followed by *Hannibal Brooks*.

He next took up the mighty challenge of *The Games*, a difficult and complex project, but a tremendously exciting one. It should be one of his greatest hits.

The next "Winner" will be his first Western, *Lawman* starring Burt Lancaster.

four Marathon runners

1
Who were these two famous singing stars of the 1930's and can you name eight films they made together?

2
What was the title of the original work on which this musical was based and who was the author?

3
Who is this star and what is the title of this musical?

4
The King And I was previously made as a non-musical. What was its title and who were its two leading players?

5
Name these three actors and the musical in which they are seen here.

6
Who was this famous singing star and in which film is he seen here? It was one of his biggest successes.

7
Two stars not usually associated with musicals sang and danced in this entertaining film. Name them and the musical.

8
Can you name ten wonderful films this famous dancing couple made together?

9
What was the name of this musical and can you remember the most famous song from it?

10
What was the title of this famous musical film?

11
What famous American conductor-composer wrote the music for this film? And what was the title?

12
The most amusing performance in this musical (that of a "dumb" silent film star) was played by which actress?

13
Name the actor dancing with Julie Andrews, the film this scene appears in and two other musicals in which he appeared.

14
This musical has been acclaimed as one of the greatest, for it proved a feast of music and dancing. What is the film?

THOSE MEMORABLE, MAGNIFICENT, MOVIE

MUSICALS

A QUIZ TO TEST YOUR MEMORY

(see answers on page 73)

DYNAMIC STREISAND

"Always I wanted to be the best. With my face, my mouth, my nose, I had to be. And I wanted to be the best everything, best singer, best actress, because I could not afford to fail," says Streisand, whose wonderful success story is told here by Betty Jennings

● Superstar. It's a word often bandied about, but to one person of only comparatively short fame it's a word that is really applicable.

That person is actress-singer Barbra Streisand. She is one of the greatest stars of today. So what has Barbra Streisand got that makes her topnotch quality?

It's certainly not her looks – even *she* admits her nose is too long and her mouth too wide – but when that electric-charged sound emits from that less than rosebud mouth and the magnetic personality switches on full blast, then you know what it is that Streisand has!

If you saw her in *Funny Girl* or *Hello, Dolly!* you'll know what I mean.

"Always I wanted to be the best," she has said. "With my face, my mouth, my nose, I had to be. And I wanted to be the best everything, best singer, best actress – nothing but the best because I could not afford to fail.

"I strive for perfection – yet part of me says 'turn off' and I do because you can't be a perfectionist all the time. That wouldn't be human and I'm not a machine.

"I have to compromise . . . a little. I know that now. I've even come to understand that a little bit of compromise is part of the perfection. Know what I mean? A little bit of imperfect is part of the perfect, because perfection is lifeless and dull."

A sense of rightness is what Barbra most certainly has.

"When I was a little kid," she has reminisced, "four, or five, I would listen to people talking and I knew they were missing each other. I couldn't tell them, but I understood it. I've always understood something or other. The realities. I sense when people are coming on, or someone does a dishonest thing or I walk into a room and something isn't right. I get it.

"I used to have just the instinctive reaction – this is right or this is wrong – and I couldn't tell why. Now I can tell why. And I'm in a position where I could easily say, 'No. Not this way.' But I hate to. It's much more satisfying to work with someone who gets it. Someone who sees it my way or can prove me wrong. I want to work with someone who can prove me wrong. It saves a lot of time.

"I always want to push right through to the basics. Sometimes I don't like myself for being so basic. I feel maybe I should be more, you know, make the small talk, be more outgoing and all that. But it wouldn't be me. I can't cope with 'You look lovely today' or 'What a pretty dress.' It makes me uncomfortable. If I dislike someone, I can't hide it. If I think an idea is lousy, I have to say so. I need someone strong to bounce off. What I hate is when I'm singing and everyone just sits there, smiling and nodding. Listen, is it good, is it bad, what is it?"

(continued overleaf)

TOP LEFT
Streisand and Michael Crawford in Hello, Dolly! *a fine musical*

TOP CENTRE
Yves Montand is her co-star in On A Clear Day You Can See Forever

TOP RIGHT
The zany Streisand in Funny Girl

FAR LEFT
The super Streisand as lovable Dolly Levi

LEFT
A scene from Funny Girl

(continued)

It's an instinct for rightness that she developed from quite an early age, this girl who considered herself rather an ugly duckling.

Born on 24th April 1942, in Brooklyn, she always felt that she wanted to be a performer.

Hers was a dream of fortune – one that came true.

As she grew older she demanded to be noticed, wearing old 1930's clothes that practically stopped the traffic.

"Sure it was the way I wanted to look," she has said. "A defence, maybe, against feeling not pretty. But it was also the dramatically right way to look. I knew it."

She won a Greenwich Village singing contest – her first step in the right direction.

The show that started her rise was the Broadway musical "I Can Get It For You Wholesale". Barbra played Miss Marmelstein, the overlooked, unloved secretary. For this role she won the "Best Supporting Actress" Award in the New York Critics' poll as well as a Tony nomination. Miss Streisand was on her way!

"Barbra has always been terribly intelligent about herself," says Herbert Ross, who choreographed "Wholesale". "The first time I met her, at the 'Wholesale' audition, she came in wearing an unbelievable racoon coat and she never stopped talking. It had to do with her not having an apartment and sleeping in somebody's office, and it was all funny and original."

"Wholesale" proved to be a fortuitous period for Barbra. She met the show's star Elliott Gould and in 1963 they married.

Elliott recalled the day she auditioned for her Miss Marmelstein role. "I sat there at the back of the stalls watching her. After her first song I knew she would be all right.

"She took off her shoes and danced around barefoot on the stage yelling 'Look, will someone phone me please? Even if I don't get the part. I've just got this phone fitted in my apartment see, and it is the first time I've had my own phone and I'd just like to have a call.'

"That night I phoned her."

They saw each other in the show and at other times, then one evening she invited him up to her apartment over a fish restaurant on Third Avenue.

"When I got there it stank so much I wouldn't go upstairs," Elliott said later.

Then they married and: "We went to live above the fish restaurant and I got used to the smell. There wasn't very much furniture and we used to eat our meals, from the top of the sewing machine. The view was pretty bleak and in the kitchen there was a rat that Barbra had named."

When the show closed Barbra was the most in-demand girl in town. Night clubs, TV, record companies, Broadway shows all put in a bid for her services. Among her fans – the late John F. Kennedy who, as the then President of the United States, invited her to perform at the White House in May 1963.

Then Barbra was offered the role of Fanny Brice in "Funny Girl" on Broadway and on the London stage. She was a tremendous hit.

When she went on to make her debut in the film version, and won an Oscar for the role, then it was obvious she deserved all the adulation.

Hello, Dolly! followed with more rave notices, to be succeeded by *On A Clear Day You Can See Forever*, some of the scenes being filmed in and around the Royal Pavilion, Brighton.

Barbra's role in *On A Clear Day* ranges from that of a young eight-year-old girl to an 18th-century lady, for in her portrayal of Daisy Gamble, gifted with extra-sensory perception, she travels back in time under hypnosis.

There are several hit tunes, including the title song, in the film that Barbra can add to her amazing repertoire.

It was while she was appearing in "Funny Girl" in the stage version that Barbra realised she was going to have a baby. Her son Jason Emanuel was born on 29th December 1966.

Unfortunately her child did not hold her marriage together, for early in 1969 she and Elliott announced "a friendly trial separation" although they said at the time "neither of us wants a divorce".

If Barbra hasn't found success in her private life she certainly has in her professional one, which doesn't always make for happiness.

As she says: "Success means something only to someone else, never to yourself. Money and success change nothing, they merely present you with a different set of problems.

"As for the money, well what is it? I limit myself to a twenty-dollar-a-week allowance. That much I can understand. Who can understand a million dollars? Nobody. There's a line in 'Funny Girl' where someone says, 'I just lost a million'. Well, someone else says, 'As long as it wasn't four dollars and ten cents.' I understand that completely. Everyone can relate to four dollars and ten cents.

"But I enjoy the work. I get a kick when I see myself in the 'rushes'. As a kid at school I would creep into the movies and watch the love scenes and think how marvellous they were and now – well, I'm doing them myself."

Barbra has come a long way from Brooklyn when she was looking for work and finding doors closed to her.

"It was degrading," she remembers. "No one should have to beg for a job. Demoralising, totally demoralising. They wouldn't audition you or even talk to you. I knew I was good. I made up my mind they'd have to come to me. 'Wait and see', I vowed. 'I'll do it on my own'."

And no one can say she hasn't done it – her way, the right way!

Barbra describes the day she became a mother as the greatest of her life. She's seen here with her son Jason

BARBRA STREISAND
(in 'Hello, Dolly!')

JAMES COBURN

ROBERT CULP and NATALIE WOOD
(in 'Bob And Carol And Ted And Alice')

FAYE DUNAWAY

PAUL NEWMAN
and
JOANNE WOODWARD

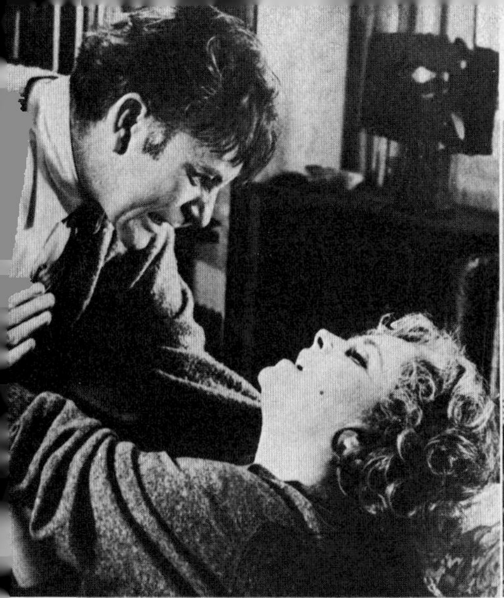

WHAT HAPPENS WHEN HUSBAND AND WIFE MAKE A MOVIE TOGETHER?

by Ian Brown

● Husband and wife "togetherness" on the screen seems to be in fashion again. Let's hope these happy couples will disprove once and for all the old Hollywood saying that if there's an Oscar on the mantelpiece, love flies up the chimney.

That particular piece of cynicism arose from the high number of marriages between actors and actresses that foundered because they tried to compete with each other professionally. And particularly when their screen paths happened to cross.

There are still several couples who refuse to act together in case it affects their marriage. Simone Signoret, for instance, has always refused to work with husband Yves Montand.

She says: "His ideas about acting differ completely from mine and we would have blazing rows if we had to work on a film together. It's better to have our private life together – and our business life completely apart."

But other famous couples have apparently taken heart from the much publicised "togetherness" of Elizabeth Taylor and Richard Burton and are allowing themselves to either appear with each other or actresses are allowing themselves to be directed by their husbands. And, with one or two exceptions, it doesn't seem to be affecting their marriages.

After her success in *Rachel, Rachel*, Joanne Woodward said: "I suppose the fact that I was being directed by my husband, and he knows me through and through, explains why, although this looked a difficult role from the script, it was the easiest part I have ever played."

Husband, of course, is Paul Newman. While they were working on *Rachel, Rachel*, the inevitable rumours cropped up about rows on the set and the possibility of them breaking up. Paul and Joanne laughed – and Paul took an advertisement in a film trade magazine to deny them.

Joanne and Paul have acted in many films together. Recently they were starred in *Winning* (as husband and wife) and Paul has just finished producing a picture called *They Might Be Giants* in which his wife stars with George C. Scott. Paul and Joanne will also be seen in *A Hall Of Mirrors*.

The gossips also keep a careful eye on Elizabeth Taylor and Richard Burton because they can't believe that two such explosive characters can work most of the time together and still stay in love. The Burtons carry it even further. If they're not acting in a film together, one always stays free of business commitments to be with the other on film locations.

As Elizabeth once said: "We just can't bear to be separated. After an hour or two apart we get restless and start looking around for each other." Liz even played an extra in Burton's *Anne Of The Thousand Days*.

Sir Laurence Olivier and his wife, actress Joan Plowright, were together in Chekov's *Three Sisters*, which Sir

TOP LEFT: The Burtons in Who's Afraid Of Virginia Woolf?

TOP RIGHT: Peter O'Toole and his wife Sian Phillips in Goodbye, Mr. Chips

ABOVE LEFT: The Oliviers, Laurence and his wife Joan Plowright appear in Three Sisters

(continued overleaf)

(continued)

Laurence directed and also starred in.

Says Joan: "I work at the National Theatre whenever possible in the same plays as Sir Laurence so that we can enjoy some home life with our children (Richard, Tamsin and Julie Kate). If I'm in a different play, then we pass each other nightly on the Brighton Belle. If I were to film, and go on location, then we'd never meet. The theatre is our basic bond. Both of us want to be working in it together. My husband and I share each other's work, but I'm strong-willed enough to sift his advice and decide for myself if I want."

Another National Theatre couple, Robert Stephens and Maggie Smith, also love working together. After their joint success in *The Prime Of Miss Jean Brodie*, they were inundated with film offers, but turned them down in favour of their first love – the stage.

Apart from her preference for the stage, Maggie is also conscious of the possible effects on her marriage if she worked regularly on films while Robert Stephens was bound up with the National Theatre.

She says: "If I was filming regularly, I'd have to be out of our flat at six in the morning and I would just be staggering home as Robert was on his way to the theatre."

But she disagrees with those who say husbands and wives shouldn't work together on the same film. "It seems like the ideal solution for show business people whose work often takes them out at different times," she says. "Robert and I thoroughly enjoyed working together on *Brodie* and being able to spend our spare time together."

Even those "wild" boys of the film sets – David Hemmings and Peter O'Toole – had the restraining influences of their wives on set with them recently in the same film.

Hemmings and his gorgeous wife Gayle Hunnicutt made *Fragment Of Fear* together, and Peter O'Toole with his wife Sian Phillips starred in *Murphy's War*. Sian was given the role after her performance with her husband in *Goodbye, Mr. Chips*, and Peter doesn't seem in the least perturbed that his wife is now coming in for as much attention from producers and the film public as he usually does himself.

In typical O'Toole fashion, he declares: "I think the reason why Sian hasn't always had loads of film offers is that she has always scared the life out of film producers. I know she scares the life out of me. . . ."

Let's wish all those husband and wife partnerships the best of luck – and let's hope they don't suffer the fate of Rod Steiger and Claire Bloom who played a husband and wife splitting up in *3 Into 2 Won't Go* – and then found soon after it was completed that their own marriage was to end.

TOP LEFT: Maggie Smith and Robert Stephens together in The Prime Of Miss Jean Brodie

TOP RIGHT: Mary Ure kissed by her husband Robert Shaw in Custer Of The West, *a large-scale Western*

ABOVE LEFT: David Hemmings and Gayle Hunnicutt go through an on-set wedding scene for Fragment Of Fear

ABOVE RIGHT: Jane Fonda and Roger Vadim, seen here making Barbarella

Christopher Plummer

ALWAYS DIFFERENT ALWAYS SUPERB!

● His latest film role is that of the Duke of Wellington in a spectacular production, *Waterloo*, in which Rod Steiger portrays Napoleon. I refer to Christopher Plummer who has played a tremendous variety of roles since he started to make films.

Consider this amazing range – the comic Lord Foppington in *Lock Up Your Daughters*; an Inca God in *The Royal Hunt Of The Sun*; the depraved Emperor Commodus in *The Fall Of The Roman Empire*; an Australian High Commissioner in *Nobody Runs Forever*; a tough fighter pilot in *Battle Of Britain*; Rommel in *The Night Of The Generals*; the secret agent Eddie Chapman in *Triple Cross*; the title role in *Oedipus The King*, as the proud, arrogant man who murders his father and marries his mother; and, of course, his most famous role of all – Baron Von Trapp in *The Sound Of Music* (though certainly not one of Plummer's own favourite portrayals!).

"For any actor, versatility is the spice of life," he says.

He's worked in films since 1956 when he made *Stage Struck*, but by then he was well known to theatre audiences for his magnificent acting in plays seen in England and America.

Born in Toronto, Canada, in 1929, he admits that his first ambition was to become a great concert pianist. But the actor in him was always present for he can remember, when taking his dog for a walk along the lakesides, he would stop "and make the dog play my straight man. I read to him from Thackeray, Dickens, Trollope, Shakespeare, Milton and others. I played kings, emperors, knights, villains, peasants, witches, conquerors, magicians. Later I took part in school plays, and at last I felt I was doing something useful and exciting – not just being a bad student."

He became a powerful force in the classical theatre, and eventually, when he felt ready, he turned to making films.

"Movies can never be an actor's medium. What he has to project is not so much his talent but the force of his personality, and he has to do it through a complex and difficult array of technical facilities."

He strongly believes his future will be as a film director. "It's very difficult to act in most films; a director's medium, the actor merely a pawn," he says. "The only way out, then, is to become a director! And I've laid my plans in this direction – writing screenplays of classics and things."

Being a firm believer in mixing intelligent classical subjects with, perhaps, more commercial stories, we can expect from him an equally exciting range of films as different as the parts he has played.

KEN JOHNS

The Fall Of The Roman Empire

The Sound Of Music

Lock Up Your Daughters

Battle Of Britain

The Royal Hunt Of The Sun

Susan George

"So far, I think everything I've ever wanted to do, I've actually done," says Susan in this feature by Betty Jennings

● One of the most persistent grouses among British actresses was always that they didn't get the good breaks in British pictures. The plum roles and films they moaned, always pivoted on the men. Think back, they'll say, can you recall when a film last centred on a woman? Well, things have changed. Many English actresses are being given tremendous chances to show us what they're made of.

Among them is Susan George who certainly can't complain about the acting roles offered her.

Although still a youngster, she was born on 26th July 1950, she's already tackled parts that many another talented actress might have wanted to get her teeth into.

Twinky was just one instance. To be cast in the important title role was fortunate, but then to have a top American actor, Charles Bronson, as your co-star – that's bounty, indeed!

But then Sue always appears to have had a guiding star.

She's the daughter of a retired musical-comedy actress and dancer known as Bubbles Percival, and a dance-band leader and saxophonist who at one time ran his own group known as "Norman George and his Music." Showbiz you might say is in Sue's blood.

Sue considers the biggest influence in her young life so far has been her mother.

"She put me on the stage as a very young child. I felt she wanted me to do all the things that she would have liked to have done in her time and never actually did. So far, I think everything I've ever wanted to do I've actually done, which is rather lovely."

This has included making her professional debut at the age of four; going to an acting school; appearing on TV in advertising commercials, serials, plays and shows; being in a West End production of "The Sound Of Music" in which she played the leading juvenile role; and making her first feature film appearance in *The Sorcerers*, starring Boris Karloff.

Small roles in *Billion Dollar Brain* and *Up The Junction* followed before her first starring role in *The Strange Affair* came about.

"I did the test on a day off from *Up The Junction* – and had raging toothache at the time. When I actually started the screen test the pain disappeared like magic – but was replaced by sheer terror!" she recalls.

The result of the test was phoned to her on her seventeenth birthday by the director of the film, David Greene.

"I realised what a super and enormous chance I'd been given," she said.

A guest role in *Looking Glass War* and another starring part in *All Neat In Black Stockings* were followed by her *Twinky* performance and then a role in *Spring And Port Wine* playing a teenager.

Today Susan has become one of the most popular young actresses on the British scene.

So there we have one very satisfied young actress who's definitely not about to join the disgruntled league.

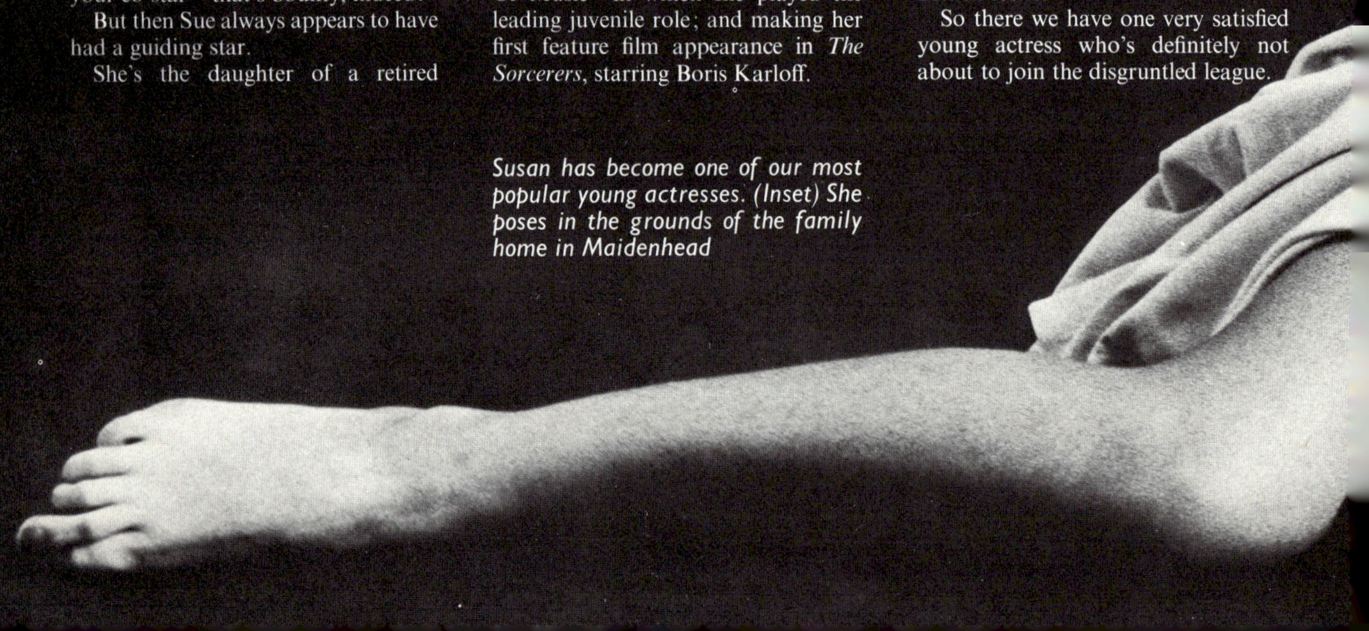

Susan has become one of our most popular young actresses. (Inset) She poses in the grounds of the family home in Maidenhead

A Last Valley

starring OMAR SHARIF and MICHAEL CAINE

● In the Austrian Tyrol, eighteen miles from Innsbruck in the beautiful Gschnitztal Valley, nestles a 17th-century village. But this is a village with a difference. Although it has farms, cottages, stables and even a church with a high tower, this village has no name, and no history. It is a film set.

It took more than 200 people with a year of research and hard work to build it at a cost of £100,000.

This nameless village is the main set for the film *A Last Valley*, produced and directed by James Clavell and starring Omar Sharif and Michael Caine.

The film is based on the story of the villagers' attempt to survive occupation by mercenary soldiers in 1641 during the dreadful Thirty Years War.

Omar Sharif plays the part of Vogel, a man who has once been a teacher. A philosophic person who values life and despairs at the chaos and destruction all around. He has been searching for sanity, but finding only death, greed and violence everywhere. Having reached a community of peasants he asks for food and lodging, but is refused.

"*The end of the world is coming*," they tell Vogel. "*Satan rules the earth and Jesus has forsaken us. We're all dead.*"

But they do not stay to tell Vogel any more. The mercenaries are coming and the peasants run for cover. Vogel hides himself in a nearby copse.

The mercenaries are cruel, tough bandits who fight on either side for money. They are led by a ruthless young Captain, played by Michael Caine.

As he watches from his hideout Vogel sees the peasants' homes smashed and fired, their possessions looted, the women raped and then murdered with the men. The Captain watches his men impassively.

Vogel escapes and runs for his life. He travels through a forest and then out into the open, where he is sickened even more by the scene. A battlefield stretches before him, dead bodies are strewn over a wide area amidst the remains of dead horses and cannons. Hanging in the air is the stench of death. Vogel, in his terror, stumbles on to his hands and knees. As he pushes himself up away from the bodies he sees that some of them are marked with the black splotches of the plague. He finds some burning wreckage, plunges his hand into the flame to cleanse it and runs screaming from the carnage.

Vogel journeys on through the ravaged countryside, passing death and destruction everywhere. When almost at an end of his strength, and starving, he suddenly emerges from the dark forest into bright sunlight. In front of him he sees a small and beautiful valley nestling in a bowl of high mountains. There he sees wheat-fields and a vineyard. He rubs his eyes in disbelief.

With the last of his strength he gropes his way down. But there are no people about. He goes to a farmhouse and knocks. There is no answer. With his knife he unfastens a shutter and slips inside then falls asleep.

He is awakened by the mercenaries. The village people have still not returned. Vogel thinks they must be working in the fields.

He is taken to the Captain. He decides that there may be a small chance of saving this village from destruction. After discussion Vogel convinces the Captain that it would be to his advantage to forget his armies outside and to spend the winter in this peaceful village where there would be food enough to keep them alive.

"*Winter's coming*," he tells the Captain. "*There's famine all over Germany. Plague, pestilence. In ten – twenty years, have you seen a richer valley? If you take their grain they starve. If you take it to your army down it goes into a thousand stomachs. Why such waste? Occupy the valley. Winter here. Live while your army dies . . . you'll never get a chance like this again.*"

Eventually the Captain realises this could indeed be a chance to save himself. He is bored with war. But the Captain

Michael Caine

Omar Sharif

Florinda Bolkan

makes the rules. Anyone breaking them or disagreeing, dies.

The mercenary soldiers have mixed feelings about sparing the village and its people. The Catholic church annoys the Protestants and they want to destroy it, but the Captain will not agree, telling them instead to build a church of their own. From then on the Captain makes it clear that there will be no more religious quarrels.

When the villagers return from their work in the fields they find their homes already occupied. They realise the only way to save themselves is to co-operate and they name Gruber (Nigel Davenport) as their spokesman.

Eventually religious and moral problems are resolved for the salvation of the community as a whole. Sacrifices have to be made and self-control administered on both sides. They all realise that life is changing. As Vogel puts it, "*The truth is that the old ways won't keep you safe anymore. The truth is that the world belongs to all of us – not to one man. Or one race. Or one religion.*"

A Last Valley and its theme of man's search for happiness began to interest producer-director and screenwriter James Clavell nine years ago when he first optioned the story which he had read as "The Fat Valley", by J. B. Pick.

The film introduces Brazilian-born Florinda Bolkan, who was awarded the much coveted feminine lead opposite Caine and Sharif. Clavell cast her for the role without a moment's hesitation after witnessing her work in two pieces of film – one a test, the other an assignment in an Italian picture.

Another comparative newcomer to films, Madeline Hinde, was given the second feminine lead portraying a peasant girl, Inge, whose hand is sought in marriage by a village youth, but who finds herself drawn to the wanderer, Vogel.

Also in the cast are Arthur O'Connell, Dudley Foster, Brian Blessed and Jack Shepherd.

SALLY FRANCIS

This Austrian village was specially built for the film

Michael Gothard as Hansen in a battle scene

Ian Hogg as Graf, Per Oscarsson as Father Sebastian, and Sharif

Michael Caine takes direction from James Clavell (with meter)

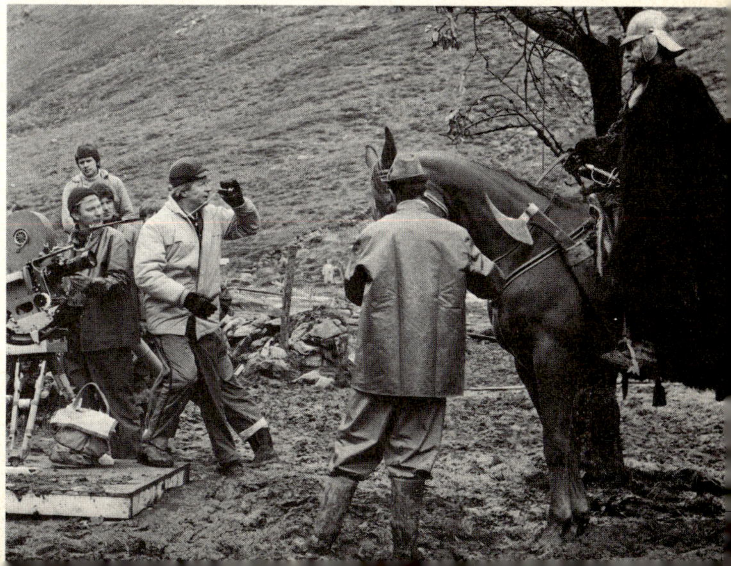

THE IMMORTALS

Judy Garland

Spencer Tracy

● Immortal is a word easily applying to the stars pictured on these and the following pages. The dictionaries give the meaning of immortal as: *Not mortal; heavenly; divine; that will not fade from memory of men; famous through all time, superhuman, gods of antiquity!* So the word certainly applies to these famous stars who were probably the greatest the cinema has ever known or will know.

They were all legends in their own lifetime.

Clark Gable, the 'King' of Hollywood as he was called, probably had the longest reign of them all. He is best remembered for his striking portrayal of Rhett Butler in *Gone With The Wind*. His was the irresistible personality that appealed to women of all ages, while their menfolk also favourably reacted to his masculinity.

Spencer Tracy, too, was in the same category. His numerous portrayals of the rough, tough man with the kindly heart endeared him to all. We last saw Spencer in *Guess Who's Coming To Dinner?* in which he starred with Katharine Hepburn. Spence and Kate had been close friends for many years.

Among the handsome-hero class we find Robert Taylor, Tyrone Power and, of course, the swashbuckling heart-breaker of them all – Errol Flynn.

All three were successful but it was Flynn's devil-may-care, happy-go-lucky attitude that won him a place in the hearts of all his fans, although his off-screen escapades often caused upheaval in Hollywood circles.

Two singers with golden voices, Mario Lanza and Judy Garland also had tempestuous careers but their fame has seldom been surpassed.

Gary Cooper and Alan Ladd epitomised the strong silent Western heroes. Coop with his slow drawl and rangy figure was the more traditional cowboy.

Perhaps the greatest of all screen tough guys was the one and only Humphrey Bogart. He could be so cynical, so villainous, but he endeared himself to an enormous amount of people.

John Garfield was yet another actor who during his short thirty-nine years made a great impact as the Tough Guy.

Known as something of a phenomenon, James Dean only made three films – *East Of Eden*, *Rebel Without A Cause* and *Giant*. However, such was his ability that the impression he made lingered on long after his disastrous death in a car accident.

Epitomising the true sex symbol was actress Marilyn Monroe. Her breathy, little-girl voice, blonde hair and wiggly walk were only a few of the attributes of this fascinating woman.

Well, will we ever see the like again of these universally popular stars?

Of course, there are many more immortals among the galaxy who are no longer with us and all had that exceptional aura, call it personality, glamour, magnetism, name what quality you will.

All were unique in their lifetimes and have remained so long after their deaths. They are the true immortals, ones that will stay captured on celluloid and forever fresh in our memories.

Robert Taylor

MARILYN MONROE

JAMES DEAN

THE IMMORTALS
(continued)

ON THIS PAGE
MARIO LANZA
CLARK GABLE
ERROL FLYNN
ALAN LADD
JOHN GARFIELD

OPPOSITE PAGE
GARY COOPER
HUMPHREY BOGART
TYRONE POWER

JACK LEMMON
(in 'The April Fools')

JACK LEMMON

A fencing bout for Jack in The April Fools

The screen's most respected light comedian has become a top movie producer. Greg Davis seeks the man behind the image...

● Jack Lemmon is surely one of the greatest of the screen's light comedy men. His films are invariably box-office hits. He made his motion picture debut in 1953 with a film called *It Should Happen To You*. He was third on the bill, following Peter Lawford and Judy Holliday. A year later he won an Academy Award for his performance in *Mister Roberts*.

Films like *The Apartment*, *Days Of Wine And Roses*, *The Odd Couple* and *The April Fools* keep him in big demand, for his countless fans realise there is no such thing as a bad film if Lemmon is listed in the credits.

However, he did once almost slip up. One of Hollywood's last big moguls, Harry Cohn, wanted Jack to appear in a film called *Joseph And His Brethren*. "When he asked I said, 'Harry, it's not me, I won't do it,' but he insisted," Lemmon said, recalling the incident.

"So I go to the studios, put on a toga and thonged sandals, and all the rest, and walk on to the set for a test. The whole crew broke up. I didn't have to do anything – they all fell about laughing as soon as they saw me.

"Anyway, I did the test and a few days later Harry called me and said, '*O.K. you did me a favour, now I'll do you one. I won't even put that test in the vaults – I'll burn it!*'"

Lemmon never did make the film.

Jack's said to be a nervous man. "I have so much nervous energy; I used to smoke several packs of cigarettes every day, but I stopped, and now I chain-smoke cigars. They keep going out, which helps, but my friends say that's because I never stop talking long enough to smoke them. Yap, yap, yap, that's me."

Few people realise that he has become as successful as a major film producer as he is an actor. "Frankly, I look forward to producing movies more than starring in them. It's a great kick to be involved in something aside from acting. There's a great feeling of accomplishment in producing, just the way there is in acting, but it is a different kind of feeling."

A Harvard graduate, Lemmon is philosophical about his career. "Boy, when I started out in acting, what wasn't I going to do. I was on my way to do two great things – save Broadway and put American music back on its feet, which it hadn't been since George Gershwin died. Unfortunately, I didn't do either, and I wound up making movies instead."

But he has much to be grateful for. Though never poor – his father was a well-to-do business man – it is unlikely that he would have ever made as much money in any other profession.

One of his important ventures was the establishing of his own production company "Jalem", which has made many films including *Days Of Wine And Roses* and *Luv*. The company's biggest success was *Cool Hand Luke* which starred Paul Newman. Although the producer's name on the credits was Gordon Carroll, Carroll is one of Jack's "Jalem" partners, and Jack was also closely involved in the production.

Jack's sixteen-year-old son, Christopher, is an accomplished musician, and Jack is pleased to see some of his own musical talent rub off on his boy. "I'm still pounding away," he says with a grin. "Since I was never successful, I've passed it on to him. He's written the music for a film I hope to direct and the producer wants it – through no exertion from me. Of course, now I can't even talk to him. He thinks he's Leonard Bernstein and Gershwin combined!"

Alec Guinness as King Charles I and Richard Harris as . . .

CROMWELL

● Just over 300 years ago, England was involved in a Civil War. For seven years, brother fought brother, neighbour fought neighbour, merchant fought aristocrat, and peasant suffered under the wave of violence.

Two men were directly responsible for the bloodshed. Both believed implicitly that they were right, and were fighting for what they believed to be God's will. On the side of the aristocracy and tradition stood King Charles the First, the most devout upholder of the Divine Right of Kings. On the side of the middle classes, demanding education for the masses, and an end to the licentious behaviour of the ruling classes was Oliver Cromwell, the man who became the first and only dictator in over 1,000 years of English history . . . against his will.

The story of this historical feud is told in an epic film in which Cromwell is played by Richard Harris. Harris had wanted to show the real man since he first became interested in the project in 1959. To some it may appear strange that an Irishman might wish to play someone whose very name still inspires hatred in Ireland after more than 300 years, but Richard felt that there was much goodness in a man maligned as evil. "He was a puritan, a devout man of God, who was moved to fight for what he believed in completely. He was a quiet, peace-loving chap, who was put in the unfortunate position of either inciting an uprising against the King, or abandoning his ideals. He chose to fight and, surprisingly, bebecame an excellent tactician and strategist."

His opponent, King Charles the First, is played by Sir Alec Guinness. An actor who has been acclaimed as "the man of a thousand faces". Guinness got right under the skin of the

execution-bound monarch, and in the film looks incredibly like the paintings we have of the King.

The film's director Ken Hughes also became interested in the story of Oliver Cromwell and Charles Stuart some years ago. He was fascinated by the inevitability of their actions, and the fact that once they committed themselves to their respective causes, there was no solution but war. One of the two had to die.

The question that haunted Hughes was, at what point do we lose control over our actions, and become controlled by them? Three years ago, Hughes began work on a screenplay for *Cromwell*, and while making *Chitty Chitty Bang Bang* he met producer Irving Allen, who also became deeply involved with the venture.

They resolved to bring the story of Cromwell to the screen. Richard Harris heard about their plans and applied for the title role. With his intense desire to play Cromwell, Hughes and Allen realised that few men would be able to bring the same authenticity to the part that Harris could muster, and decided to use him. When Guinness agreed to play Charles, all was set for a gigantic movie production.

The location site was chosen. Spain was the choice. Parts of Spain are incredibly like the green rolling hillside country of England, but are fortunately uncluttered by electricity pylons and television aerials. The Spanish army agreed to loan 400 trained soldiers to play the respective armies of the feuding politicians.

Dozens of horses had to be trained for the stunt sequences, in which thousands of men and horses had to be "blown up" by cannon and mutilated in hand-to-hand combat.

Whatever one thinks of Cromwell – and everyone must make up his own mind – the film sets out to be entirely honest. The characters have been played as they probably really were, with no concessions made for glamour or excitement. Many of us must wonder what motives charged the two men who changed the course of our history. This is the story of *Cromwell*.

GREG DAVIS

George Lazenby from commercials and Diana Rigg from "The Avengers" in On Her Majesty's Secret Service

"Peyton Place" stars: Mia Farrow, Ryan O'Neal and Barbara Parkins

FROM TV FAME TO MOVIES

by Ian Brown

Roger Moore is now making feature films again

● Television can hardly be described as the film industry's best friend, but it *has* had one beneficial side effect.

Many of the big names in films today have graduated from the small screen to the big screen – and taken their fans with them. People like Roger Moore, Robert Vaughn, Richard Chamberlain, Mia Farrow, Robert Culp and many others became household names all over the world because of television series in which they appeared and are now repeating their success on the big screen.

But why don't they just stick to television, where the financial rewards are often as high and the work sometimes not so arduous?

The big attraction is the variety of roles artists can play in films after being confined to the one character on television. Richard Chamberlain used to complain about Dr. Kildare: "That guy's so good that he's boring. The trouble is that I've grown up and the Kildare character hasn't. And the fans expect you to be the same off-screen as you are on. Fancy trying to live up to an image like Kildare's."

Chamberlain has, since leaving his TV series, played a role in *Julius Caesar*, and a more complex character – the composer Tchaikovsky – in *The Lonely Heart*.

Robert Vaughn found the confines of Napoleon Solo's character in "The Man from UNCLE" increasingly irksome and Roger Moore towards the end didn't express himself in saintly terms about "The Saint", though he is eternally grateful for the role which made him a top star. Both Moore and Vaughn were sensible enough to learn all they could about the techniques and financial structures of film-making while engaged on their television series.

Roger Moore once gave me another reason why top television stars are always anxious to try their luck on the bigger screen. "An awe of film stars and film-making was so deeply established when we were young and before there was any

Patrick McGoohan left his "Danger Man" days behind for films

Robert Culp of "I Spy"

David Janssen came to fame in "The Fugitive"

This was James Garner back in his "Maverick" days on TV

Richard Chamberlain, no longer Dr. Kildare, as Octavius in Julius Caesar

television, that an actor doesn't really feel he has hit the big time until he has been a success in films. The glamour of the film industry – for the star as well as for the public – is still very strong."

Like Roger Moore many of today's stars had been in the film business for years before a success in a popular television series catapulted them to international fame.

Richard Crenna, for example, started acting at the age of ten and had an impressive, but unnoticed, list of film supporting roles to his name before being starred in television's "Slattery's People". Now he is in great demand by the film-makers for leading roles. You may remember him in *Star!* and *Marooned*. He also played a top role in *The Sand Pebbles*.

Actresses have also found television success a passport to film stardom. Before "Peyton Place" who had ever heard of Mia Farrow? Now she can pick and choose her films. Other stars from "Peyton Place", Barbara Parkins and Ryan O'Neal, are now making big movies.

The "Avengers" girls Honor Blackman and Diana Rigg found a rich consolation on the big screen after their spells of helping Patrick Macnee on the small screen had come to an end. Macnee himself is also making big feature films.

There have been rich film pickings, too, for the television cowboys. The years spent in the saddle by James Garner, Clint Eastwood and Clint Walker in series are paying off.

We even have television to thank for the big-screen James Bonds. It was Sean Connery's performance in a television play "Requiem For A Heavyweight" that led to him being cast as Bond. In the play, he was a boxer – a part that showed off to advantage his physical, as well as acting, attributes.

And, of course, there was George Lazenby, who was the star of a major commercial advert on the small screen, but ended up an even bigger star when he took on the role of Bond for *On Her Majesty's Secret Service*. . . .

The one woman in his life – wife Neile

Action is Steve's "thing"

Steve, the movie producer

● One actor who has never been part of the Hollywood crowd, and doesn't mind admitting it, is masculine, sophisticated rebel Steve McQueen.

People praise him, the "in" people want him to join them, fans give him adulation, but McQueen is essentially a loner.

"I live for myself," he says in the hesitant way he uses when trying not to give away his private, guarded self. "I answer to nobody and I'm not trying to sound pompous or anything like that, but I live for myself and I feel that I have no obligations to answer to anybody for anything."

Philosophically he adds, "The world is as good as you are. You've got to learn to like yourself first."

It's more usual to find Steve behind the wheel of a car

THE STEVE McQUEEN STORY

One of Hollywood's most dynamic stars believes in living life to the full. Betty Jennings tells the story behind his rise to international acclaim

The loneliness started way back in his youth. His parents separated and he was brought up on a farm in Missouri by his grandparents, and there were times when he wasn't good and didn't like himself.

Steve had a few encounters with the law and ended up in a reform school.

He says today of his restless youth: "I had a chip on my shoulder; I was getting into trouble, and as I think back, I was fortunate not to get into any serious trouble with the authorities."

About this time the urge to move on caused him to get various jobs that took him far and wide. He took, among other jobs, work as a deck-hand on a Greek oil-tanker, worked in the oilfields of Texas, in a carnival and was a tree-lopper in a Canadian lumber camp for a time.

Then he enlisted in the Marine Corps where he became a tank driver and mechanic and so gained a love for anything with an engine.

On his discharge from the Marines he again tried any job going until he landed in Greenwich Village and became intrigued by the artistic people who congregated there. An actress friend suggested he try acting. He laughed at the idea at first, but fate moves in strange ways and he was accepted as a student by the Actors Studio in New York.

His first big break came with TV's "Wanted Dead Or Alive" series as bounty hunter Josh Randall.

Other milestones in his career have included his role in the films *Never So Few*, *The Magnificent Seven*, *The Great Escape*, *Nevada Smith*, *The Sand Pebbles* (it earned him an Oscar nomination and he considers it his favourite film) and *The Thomas Crown Affair*.

Established as a star Steve set up Solar Productions with his partner Bob Relyea – they wanted to make realistic films filled with adventure and their first, *Bullitt*, hit the success jackpot.

He did his own stunt driving. "They wanted to shoot the *Bullitt* chase inside the studio lot. It wouldn't have kidded anybody. I'm not a phoney and I don't want to be connected with anything that is. So I said we shoot it in the actual San Francisco streets or we don't shoot it at all.

"Those sequences for *Bullitt* were the hairiest thing I have

A romantic interlude in his latest film, The Reivers

ever done," he adds. And this is from the man who in the past has thought nothing of competing in international car race events and in the early 1960's was a member of the USA team in the famous International Six-Day Trial motorcycle races in East Germany.

"I don't figure I'm anything so special with motorcycles," he says, "but I do it because I need it. You ought to understand this about me and motorcycle riding. I've lived in a very close world, and I've tried very hard while I was racing to keep

(continued overleaf)

"The world is becoming too chaotic. Everyone is rushing and running until they have nowhere to go," says Steve.

(continued)

cameras away and public relations people away, because it's my private world, and I do feel strongly about it."

While making *The Reivers* on location he took two motorcycles with him. He claims driving is a form of mental therapy – it relaxes him.

The Reivers is based on William Faulkner's Pulitzer Prize-winning novel (the title means a rascal and a rogue) and playing head reiver? You guessed it, Steve McQueen.

Somewhat a change of pace for the star – it recounts a journey undertaken with a young boy from Mississippi to Memphis in the early 1900's.

"It's a happy picture. One that has a wealth of humour and action," he says.

Action, too, is in the forefront with his latest two movies for his company Solar Productions.

He comes into his own "thing" with *Le Mans*, an adventure-drama set against the background of the famous twenty-four-hour car race, while *Man On A Nylon String*, another project, is a mystery adventure story about mountaineers who attempt to conquer Switzerland's giant Eiger.

Steve has received many injuries through his love of speed and hazardous filming methods, but now says: "I have definitely started to change gear, to slow down.

"The world is becoming too chaotic, everyone is rushing and running, until they have nowhere else to go. And worse, nothing left to give to yourself."

Steve is very much an individualist and has decided views on how he wants to live.

"I think if everyone could just go away for a few hours a day, there would be no need for psychiatrists or therapists or all the doctors who have to treat people for nervous conditions brought on by the perpetual whirlwind of the kind of world we've created for ourselves. If you give yourself time during the day to unravel your thoughts, to put your mind back into focus, you're able to maintain a healthy mental balance with yourself."

His wife, Neile, they married on 2nd November 1956, will no doubt be pleased to hear him mention the slowing-down bit – if it ever happens!

She has long advocated he do so and tried to impress him with his family responsibilities – they have two children Terry Leslie, born 5th June 1959, and Chadwick Steve, born 28th December 1960.

Steve says: "If I take too many chances Neile gives me hell. But there are many people living more dangerously than me. Besides she knows how much I enjoy it.

"On the other hand, if I go too fast and I get my heart in my throat I think of the hard time I'm going to get when I get home, and I slow down.

"I have a wife, two kids, an old Spanish home and a couple of acres. Man, I am happy. I have always tried to be honest with myself and because of it I have had to take my lumps. But I made the breakthrough."

TOP: "I live for myself and I feel that I have no obligations to answer to anybody for anything"

ABOVE: His wife Neile was an actress before she married Steve

LEFT: Steve with Faye Dunaway in The Thomas Crown Affair

STEVE McQUEEN

GLEN CAMPBELL
(in 'True Grit')

OMAR SHARIF

CLINT EASTWOOD
(in 'Kelly's Heroes')

CLINT

He broke through as "The Man With No Name" and today the name Clint Eastwood means big business at the box office

by Betty Jennings

● If he were introduced as "The Man With No Name" most people would instantly recognise the tall, lean handsome man and he would be accepted, even acclaimed.

Why, you might ask?

Well, it was but a few years ago that a rugged American actor went to Italy and really made a name for himself with several "spaghetti" Westerns, as they became known.

The actor was affectionately dubbed by the Italians – "El Cigarillo" for his role as "The Man With No Name" in those Westerns and, as is so often said, became an overnight success.

And thereby hangs a story.

The story of Clint Eastwood, the actor in question, who only really found big success on going to foreign shores.

Clint was born 31st May 1930, in San Francisco, the son of Clint and Ruth Eastwood. As a child he moved with his parents (his father is a company executive) to Oakland just across the bay from his birthplace. Clint has a younger sister, Jeanne.

At school he was the star of the basketball team and completely disinterested in dramatics.

On graduating he worked for a time as a lumberjack in Oregon before going into the army.

His fitness stood him in good stead on one occasion. He was making a trip by naval plane when it developed engine trouble and plunged into the water. The pilot had a lifejacket, but Clint didn't and so he had to swim until he reached the shore which was, luckily, only four miles away. "In camp I taught the soldiers swimming and so I was in good form," he says. "Those four miles were not too tiring. The six-mile walk from

(continued overleaf)

"People said I was a great type for Westerns," says Clint

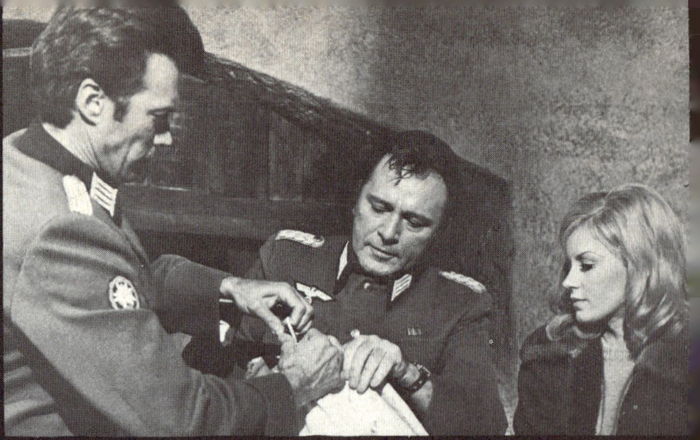

(continued)

the shore to the nearest village was far more taxing!"

He entered Los Angeles City College on his discharge from the army and while there Universal Studios offered him a contract. Small parts followed, but it was not until he was seen one day at CBS Television City by Robert Sparks, then a CBS executive producer, that his first break came. Sparks had been discussing casting problems for a TV series called "Rawhide". He came out of an office and saw Clint standing in a doorway. A few minutes later Clint had an appointment to read for the role – which he won, and so began his long stint, of nearly eight years in the successful TV series.

This sort of coincidence, or little bit of luck, has often occurred to Clint. As he says: "Me? I've been lucky. That's not to say I didn't work hard at it, but I believe there's luck involved in it, too. There were the lean years in which I knocked my brains out trying. People said I was a great type for Westerns. Any time anyone is over six feet tall, they're told they are a great type for Westerns. Sure I was the rangy type. I don't know if cowboys were really that tall in the 1800's, but the Gary Coopers and the John Waynes set the precedent over the years.

"In 'Rawhide' I did get awfully tired of playing the conventional white hat. The hero who kisses old ladies and dogs and was kind to everybody. I decided it was time to be an anti-hero."

So then came Clint's next spot of luck. Italian movie-maker Sergio Leone, a Western fan, was looking for an actor to take the lead of "The Man With No Name" in *A Fistful Of Dollars*. He saw Clint in his TV role and sent him the script.

No one was more surprised than Clint when the film brought him instant international success.

For A Few Dollars More and *The Good, The Bad And The Ugly* followed. They were often unneccessarily violent, but they made a tremendous amount of money.

Clint's trademarks were a poncho blanket over his shoulders, a hat

TOP LEFT: In a scene from Where Eagles Dare *with Richard Burton and Mary Ure*

TOP RIGHT: Clint chats with Alan Jay Lerner, producer of Paint Your Wagon

LEFT: Clint with the late Eric Fleming in their popular "Rawhide" days

ABOVE: War is the theme of his new film Kelly's Heroes

RIGHT: In Paint Your Wagon *Clint played his first movie singing role as well as light comedy*

pulled down over his eyes, and the butt of a cigarillo hanging from the corner of his mouth – hence his nickname "El Cigarillo". He played the hard-eyed, unshaven stranger, a deadly shot with his ever-ready six-shooter, and with an over-abundant talent for trouble, who rode in from nowhere, a rough, tough desperado, ever ready to kill.

"In the *Dollar* films, 'stoic' was the word. It was stoicism against comedic things. It was comedy and yet it was played dead straight," he says.

"The violence tag was hung too tightly around my neck. The fact that they were made by an Italian in Europe had some people going in edgy as I was when I made them. I personally don't think of them as violent, only perhaps, as black humour."

He made *The Witches*, *Coogan's Bluff*, *Hang 'Em High* and *Where Eagles Dare*, the latter an exciting movie with Richard Burton as his co-star, before taking a complete change of pace with the musical comedy *Paint Your Wagon*. Lee Marvin and Jean Seberg were his co-stars in this.

"*Paint Your Wagon* opened things up for me," he said at the time. "It got me back out of all the anti-heroics. I sang in it and played a lot of light comedy, too. The range was from almost farce to a deep and tender poignancy. It was also a very romantic role when you recall there was no romance to the *Dollar* films at all. Not even women involved. As to my singing, I'll let the public be the judge of that.

"Singing has never been my foremost thing. I did make an album about seven years ago and about four singles. They weren't the talk of the airways, particularly, but I had taken lessons. The records met with moderate success.

"Like every TV actor, I thought I'd try singing, so I made a few records. I hoped they might make the top of the record charts, which they didn't, but I had no idea I'd be a singing leading man.

"I sang 'I Talk To The Trees' and 'I Still See Eliza' as solos and quite a few more with the cast in *Wagon*. It's all our voices without a lot of tricked up electronics, which is nice. Pardner (the character I play) is down to earth, introspective, quiet, partially a wistful dreamer. It was definitely time for a change of pace and I needed him when he got here. A little bit of luck, again."

His latest films include another Western, *Two Mules For Sister Sara*, with Shirley MacLaine, and a war subject titled *Kelly's Heroes*.

We hear comparatively little about Clint's private life. Perhaps because little publicity has been given to his happy marriage of fifteen years. Maggie, his wife, a former model, presented Clint with a son, Kyle Clinton, born in May 1968.

For relaxation Clint enjoys playing golf, fishing, swimming, tennis and motorcycling – with Maggie often riding pillion.

"He loves tracking down on Big Sur on his bike," says Maggie, "and rides into San Francisco if the mood takes him."

Sean Connery is a keen golfer

James Garner caught the speed bug while filming Grand Prix

STARS OFF THE SET

HOW DO THE STARS SPEND THEIR SPARE TIME AWAY FROM THE SET? IAN BROWN HAS BEEN FINDING OUT

Clint Eastwood is a motorcycle enthusiast

A game of chess for Patrick McGoohan

Anthony Quinn – a keen chess player inbetween scenes for Nobody Loves Flapping Eagle

Steve McQueen is almost addicted to machinery

Mike Caine and Omar Sharif enjoy a card game

Elke Sommer's hobby is painting. A great deal of her work has been exhibited

● Omar Sharif has gone on record that he'd rather be known as a top bridge player than as a film star.

Away from the movie sets, many film and TV stars have shown passionate interests in various sports.

Jack Palance, for instance, was a boxer before he became an actor. By the age of twenty-one, he had fought twenty-two professional bouts and lost only two of them. Steve McQueen was a professional motorcyclist, Sean Connery has become an intensely keen golfer and Charlton Heston, a tennis player of exceptional ability, plays regularly with the top names in the game.

This era of the sporting stars is indicative of the changed times in the film world. Twenty years ago, top stars wouldn't have dared play a violent sport in case their precious profiles were dented. Now that rugged looks are "in" the stars are often allowed to indulge their various tastes in sport.

The only people who worry are the insurance companies. Steve McQueen is still so fanatical about speed that insurance companies refuse to cover him when he's working on a film. You can hardly blame them when Steve's idea of relaxing after a day on the set is to get his head down over the wheel and race around at speeds of over 100 mph.

Another star who has become addicted to speed is James Garner. This followed his role in *Grand Prix* when he insisted on doing the driving himself.

He says: "I didn't understand what guys saw in motor racing and when I started the film I asked to drive myself as a matter of honour more than anything else. Then it got into my blood and now I make for a race track whenever I can."

Clint Eastwood goes in for long-distance running to keep his body in trim. He's up at the crack of dawn most days to trot "a mile or two to wake myself up." Clint also loves speeding around on a motorcycle.

As you would imagine from their build, Sean Connery and his brother Neil, did a lot of boxing in their younger days. Surprisingly, from his build, Norman Wisdom is another star with trophies for boxing on his sideboard. Norman was the bantam and fly-weight champion of the 11th Hussars in India during the war, and it was boxing that led to him becoming a comedian.

If he was so much on top of his opponent that the fight was becoming a bore, Norman used to clown around by doing the acrobatic falls and gormless facial expressions for which he is now famous. The laughter he got from the troops then convinced him that he had a better future on the stage than he had in a boxing ring.

Tommy Steele is among the British stars who were almost tempted to take up football instead of show business. He and other top names still enjoy their outings with a Show Business XI playing matches for charity.

But it is golf that claims the off-screen attention of most stars. Most use it as a means of relaxation, but many are top-class players who could hold their own in any golfing company. Bob Hope and Bing Crosby are old rivals on the golf course as well as on screen, and before he became keen on motor racing James Garner was perhaps the best of the American show business golfers. He entered for the British Open Championship in 1962 but had to withdraw at the last moment because of a film commitment.

The top British golfer is probably Christopher Lee, who still goes round in the low seventies even though he doesn't play regularly now. Before he became an international star, he won several amateur tournaments. Chris also has trophies for athletics, fencing and boxing. It was because of this all-round prowess that he came into show business—as a stunt man.

DARLING JULIE

LESLIE WILKINSON DISCUSSES THE LIFE AND CAREER OF LOVELY JULIE ANDREWS

● Somehow one is always inclined to think of Julie Andrews as being associated only with singing and musicals, forgetting that in her non-musical films she has proved to be a more than competent actress.

After all, she had first been presented to the British public at the London Hippodrome in 1947 at the age of twelve in a revue called "Starlight Roof". She was introduced by the star of the show, Vic Oliver, and immediately burst forth into an operatic aria which "brought down the house". She had studied singing not only with the famous opera singer Madame Stiles-Allen, but also with her stepfather Ted Andrews who, with her mother Barbara, was also in the show.

Then, in 1954, she had made her bow on Broadway in Sandy Wilson's "The Boy Friend", following this with two

In her new film, *Darling Lili*, Julie Andrews portrays

TOP LEFT
It's romance for Julie and Rock Hudson in Darling Lili, her new film

TOP RIGHT
Julie's greatest screen hit, The Sound Of Music

LEFT
Robert Wise who directed Julie in The Sound Of Music and Star! presents her with a Photoplay "Best Actress" Award

years as Eliza in "My Fair Lady", continuing in this role for a further eighteen months in London and then returning to Broadway for "Camelot". The accumulated earnings of the last-named shows were seventeen million dollars!

The disappointment at not being selected for the screen version of "My Fair Lady" was soon replaced by the happiness that must have been Julie's at the huge success of *Mary Poppins* (1964), her first starring film and the one which won her worldwide acclaim. *The Americanisation Of Emily* (1964) caused some surprise as Julie didn't sing in this, but she was back in all her vocal glory in *The Sound of Music* (1965).

Torn Curtain (1966) and *Hawaii* (also 1966) were both acting vehicles in which Julie showed that she was something

(*continued overleaf*)

a British singer who leads a double life—she's a spy!

TOP: In Darling Lili *Julie plays a spy!*

CENTRE LEFT: She portrayed Gertrude Lawrence in Star!

CENTRE RIGHT: Paul Newman was her co-star in a Hitchcock thriller, Torn Curtain

ABOVE: In the musical Thoroughly Modern Millie *she was partnered by Mary Tyler Moore and Carol Channing*

(continued)

more than just a pretty voice . . . but somehow these two films were soon forgotten, because all through the periods of their release *The Sound Of Music* was continuing to triumph and break records wherever it played.

Thoroughly Modern Millie (1967) gave Julie another shot in the arm (as if she really needed it!), singing and dancing once more into the hearts of her fans. And then came *Star!*

All the previous films (including the non-singing ones) had proved themselves big money-makers and yet *Star!* somehow missed. It gave Julie a chance to sing and act, both of which she did most admirably and it also showed her great versatility in the variety of songs presented. Maybe it had nothing to do with Julie and people were just not interested in, or were just plain ignorant of Gertrude Lawrence, the star portrayed by Julie in the film.

Perhaps it would have been more popular if it had not been angled at one particular star. Perhaps the fans, with that extrasensory perception one has regarding those in whom one takes a special interest – rather like the concern one might have for a well-loved friend – began to wonder if Julie was losing that girlish effervescent sparkle.

Still, it's no use surmising. *Star!* was born (and faded) and *She Loves Me* and *Say It With Music* (two other projects for Julie) were, to use a similar metaphor, strangled at birth.

Which brings us to *Darling Lili*, yet another combination of the two things Julie does best: singing *and* acting. The film has a World War I background set in Paris, London, Berlin and behind German military lines, and Lili is a British singing entertainer who is leading a double life.

In the London of 1915 she is the favourite star of soldiers on leave and helping to boost the morale of those fighting the war on the home front . . . but Lili is also a clever and cool-headed German spy, whose activities are entirely above suspicion as she mingles with military personnel, socialites and theatrical personalities.

Her main quarry is an Allied air squadron commander (played by Rock Hudson), from whom she aims to get information regarding important troop and aerial movements. *But* (you've guessed it!) she falls madly in love with him, which completely disrupts her spying activities . . . and there is a suspense-packed denouement to the film which takes place in a Zeppelin bound for Germany.

With new songs by Henry Mancini, plus popular standards of World War I (which proved such a big feature of *Oh! What A Lovely War*), put over by Julie as only she knows how – *and* a plot which involves her as a svelte, Ninotchka-type lady in intriguing love battles with Rock Hudson – this could be the winner to eclipse all Julie's previous great successes.

Anyway, the whole delectable mixture is in the hands of the person most fitted for the task: Blake Edwards, the writer-producer-director whose many hits in this trio of capacities include *Breakfast At Tiffany's* (1961), *The Pink Panther* (1963), *A Shot In The Dark* (1964) and *The Great Race* (1965). He wrote (with William Blatty) the script of *Darling Lili*, he produced it and he directed it.

What is more, in November 1969 he married Julie Andrews.

JULIE ANDREWS

GOLDIE HAWN

GOLDIE'S YEAR...!

She's the girl who giggled her way through "Laugh-In" to Movies

● When a girl says that one of her earliest memories is of running through her city backyard naked, as a cherub, it tends to place her in a certain category.

And when I tell you the girl who made the statement is the blonde, blue-green huge-eyed, scatterbrained Goldie Hawn you'll know what I mean.

Goldie is the doll-like, daffy female who made an impact with her zany mannerisms in "Rowan and Martin's Laugh-In" on TV and is now currently making films. *Cactus Flower*, her first starring movie, won her an Oscar.

But let's go back twenty-odd years and see what has happened to young Goldie Hawn (her real name) up until her present age.

She's the daughter of Edward Rutledge Hawn and his wife, Laura, of Washington, USA. Her father is a professional musician.

Goldie began taking ballet and tap-dancing lessons at the age of three, adding modern jazz dancing to her repertoire at the age of eleven.

This led, in her later teens, to her operating a successful dancing school with some 150 pupils eager to follow in her footsteps.

But in the evenings Goldie was continuing her drama studies, which she had concentrated on at university, and one could say she was getting itchy to branch out along these lines.

Consequently, when an offer came for her to join the chorus of a group entertaining at New York's World Fair, Goldie jumped at the opportunity.

"I was dancing the can-can, doing lotsa kicks, showing lotsa leg," she says of those days.

Other tours followed in repertory with shows such as "Kiss Me Kate" and "Guys And Dolls". One trip was to Puerto Rico where she appeared in the chorus of a revue.

Eventually she auditioned for work on TV and got a dancing spot on an Andy Griffith TV Special.

This was when agent Art Simon "saw something special" in her and pushed her forward until that something special paid off as her resident giggler role in "Laugh-In".

Who could help but be tickled pink by the "dumb blonde" characterisation from a girl who had such silly lines to say and then usually fluffed them!

Her comment about her public image is probably not far from the truth. "She's a kind of fantasy figure, the totally helpless little girl that some men dream about. Women don't regard her as competition because she's so frothy they know she can't really be like that.

"Really, I have no particular goal," she says. "I'm drifting along following the line of least resistance. Sure, I have ambition, but not a driving kind of ambition like, say, a man in business."

Cactus Flower has put her on the pathway to films, and Mike Frankovich, executive producer of the film, thinks highly enough of her to star her in *There's A Girl In My Soup*, with Peter Sellers, and there are two more pictures lined up for this dizzy, talented comedienne.

Happily married to producer Gus Trikonis and with a good film career ahead of her it certainly has been Goldie's year!

BETTY JENNINGS

TOP LEFT: Goldie's first movie starring role – opposite Ingrid Bergman in Cactus Flower

TOP RIGHT: Goldie with her husband Gus Trikonis

LEFT: In London Goldie attended the premiere of Marooned and met Lord Mountbatten and Gregory Peck

NEW FACES

GENEVIEVE BUJOLD

Genevieve Bujold is the girl who captured wonderful notices for her role of Anne Boleyn in *Anne Of The Thousand Days*. The twenty-six-year-old French-Canadian spent twelve years at a convent school before joining the Montreal Conservatory of Drama. Whilst still at the school, Genevieve was offered a part and took it, but it meant losing her diploma. "A diploma can't get a girl an acting start . . . a part can," she said defiantly. Before *Anne*, she appeared in seven films, all French-speaking, two of which were directed by her husband Paul Almond, one of Canada's leading young film-makers. She now looks set for great success.

RICHARD BENJAMIN

Richard Benjamin made his screen debut in *Goodbye, Columbus*. He was born in New York and toured in several plays before appearing on Broadway in "The Star Spangled Girl". He is married to Paula Prentiss and starred with her in the amusing TV series "He and She". His next feature film is *Diary Of A Mad Housewife*.

ALI MacGRAW

Ali MacGraw, one of America's top fashion models, made her film debut in *Goodbye, Columbus*. She was born in Westchester County, N.Y. and has appeared in numerous TV commercials and in the pages of many top fashion magazines. She won her film role from among more than 100 actresses and unknowns. Her next film is *Love Story*.

SINEAD CUSACK

A twenty-one-year-old on the verge of stardom, Sinead is the daughter of actor Cyril Cusack. Born in Dublin, she left university six months before her finals to join the Abbey Theatre Company playing every sort of role. She had two small film roles, in *David Copperfield* and *Tam Lin*, before breaking through and getting the starring female role in *Hoffman*, opposite Peter Sellers. Now her future is assured.

ELLIOTT GOULD

Elliott Gould is six foot three inches. He was born in Brooklyn, and claims he can't ever remember wanting to be anything but an actor. His first film was *The Night They Raided Minskys*. He made his name with his second, *Bob And Carol And Ted And Alice*, and now Elliott appears in *Getting Straight*, *M.A.S.H.*, *Move* and is set to star in many more.

GENEVIEVE GILLES

Beautiful French ex-model Genevieve Gilles made her feature film debut in *Hello-Goodbye*, starring Michael Crawford. Her first ambition was to become a lawyer, but her looks were against her. Admirers told her it would be a shame to waste her beauty in a courtroom, so she started fashion modelling. Her movie break came when a documentary was made about fashion, and Genevieve had the leading part. The film was successful, and her face became noticed in the film world. "I suppose you might say I'm a determined girl," she says. "I very much want to succeed in films and I am willing to work hard to achieve this. What I need as well, but what nobody can give me, is luck."

JOANNA LUMLEY

A highly successful model, Joanna's first film was *On Her Majesty's Secret Service*. She followed up with *Tam Lin*, with Ava Gardner. Now the stunning beauty is starring in *The Breaking Of Bumbo*, which offers her a most important role. She was born in India, and educated in a convent here. She has a two-year-old son, James.

RICHARD WARWICK

Twenty-four-year-old Richard made his debut in the Zefferelli version of *Romeo And Juliet*, and followed that by playing one of Malcolm MacDowell's sidekicks in *If*. From this he went on to *The Bed-Sitting Room*, and then to Hungary for *First Love*. He plays the male lead role in *The Breaking Of Bumbo*.

NATASHA PYNE

Natasha is probably best known for her role in the TV series "Father, Dear Father" but she has been working in television since 1962. The twenty-three-year-old actress made her start in movies with *The Taming Of The Shrew*, and has since appeared in several other films, the latest being *The Breaking Of Bumbo*.

NEW FACES

BRUCE DAVISON • CATHY BURNS • RICHARD THOMAS • BARBARA HERSHEY

The four young stars of *Last Summer* achieved big success. Bruce Davison, whose first film this was, had almost given up hope of achieving anything actor-wise when this golden opportunity came along. Cathy Burns was born in New York City and after studying at the American Academy of Dramatic Arts won a leading role in a TV production of Arthur Miller's "The Crucible". In the Broadway production "The Prime of Miss Jean Brodie" she was spotted by Frank and Eleanor Perry, director and writer respectively of *Last Summer*. Richard Thomas began acting at the age of six and in the next nine years appeared in numerous repertory productions. He co-starred in his own TV series and featured in seven others. It was while Barbara Hershey was a student at Hollywood High School that she got her first break in a "Gidget" TV episode, which later led to a serial role as Kathy in "The Monroes". She graduated to feature films (*With Six You Get Eggroll* and *Heaven With A Gun*) and will next be seen in *The Baby Makers*.

DON SCARDINO

Don Scardino was born in New York City twenty-one years ago and is considered one of the most talented youngsters to emerge in recent years. His parents, both musicians of merit, have endowed him with considerable artistic verve. He has appeared in countless stage productions and television shows and now makes his film debut in *Homer*. He is a talented vocalist and guitarist and has made several records. Don wrote and recorded three songs especially for *Homer*.

WENDELL BURTON

Wendell Burton, who co-starred with Liza Minnelli in *Pookie* was born in San Antonio, Texas, but when he was fourteen his family moved to Novato, thirty miles north of San Francisco. From cashier in a supermarket (with ambitions for a political career) he was persuaded by the college professor who was teaching him public speaking to take up drama, which he did, winning the lead in the stage show, "You're A Good Man, Charlie Brown."

ARLO GUTHRIE

He was born in Coney Island, New York, on 10th July 1947. The son of one of the world's most famous folk-singers, Woody Guthrie, Arlo has been singing and playing since he was a child. The Guthrie home was always filled with the big names of folk and blues, and Arlo learned from them all. His film *Alice's Restaurant* was based on his song of the same name. He became, almost overnight, an idol of hippies.

BARRY NEWMAN

Barry Newman, who made his motion picture debut in *The Lawyer*, was born in Boston, Massachusetts, and as a teenager had no ambition to be an actor, but intended to become a jazz musician. Then, one day at Columbia University, he attended an acting class and was immediately "hooked". Soon after leaving college he landed a featured role in a Broadway musical "What Makes Sammy Run?", followed by four other Broadway shows and a TV programme called "Edge Of Night".

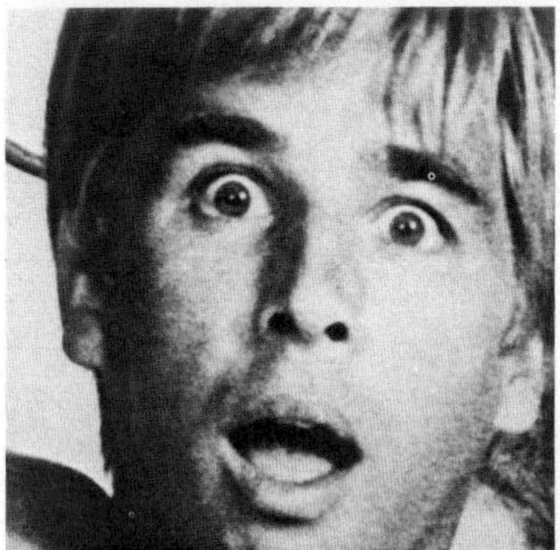

BEAU BRIDGES

Beau is the son of Lloyd Bridges. He became an actor almost by accident. He made his movie debut in a film called *The Red Pony* at the age of five, but he gave up acting because he was more interested in baseball. He started acting again whilst at college, and after graduating he went into TV, before appearing in *The Incident* and *For Love Of Ivy*. His big film break came in *Chicago, Chicago* with Melina Mercouri. His next picture is titled *The Christian Liquorice Store*.

KIM DARBY

The charming star who made such a hit in *True Grit* was born in Hollywood on 8th July 1948. She is 5 feet 6 inches, weighs 113 lbs. and has dark brown eyes and hair. She won her first success in TV. Kim has made three other films: *A Time For Giving*, *Norwood* and *The Strawberry Statement*. We can expect to see her in many more.

JOHN WAYNE in CH

Chisum (Wayne) and his enemy Murphy (Forrest Tucker) have an epic fight over epic stakes

● He's an incredible star in every true sense of the word. John Wayne I'm talking about. At sixty-two, with only one lung, here he is again in a role that demands much physical action from him, and Wayne rises to every dangerous challenge as though he were fresh out of an acting school. Anyone who thinks his saddle days are over better not repeat it to Wayne. Movies are his life and they've been so for the last forty years.

His outstanding movie record as a top box-office star, his countless thrilling Westerns, his big-heartedness and his courage have all helped to make him one of Hollywood's greatest stars, loved and respected in every corner of the world.

Now comes his 201st film, and it's *another* Western. This one is titled *Chisum*, and is based on an exciting part of the life of John Simpson Chisum, known as the "King of the Pecos" who initiated America's westward cattle drives in the 1870's.

The time is 1878 and Chisum, owner of a vast and sprawling New Mexico ranch, is waiting for the arrival of his pretty niece, Sallie (Pamela McMyler) from the East. While he and his sidekick, Pepper (Ben Johnson) are waiting for the stagecoach, a group of Mexican rustlers raid his horses, killing several of Chisum's men. In town Chisum meets Murphy (Forrest Tucker) who is trying to dominate the land, foreclosing farm mortgages, refusing to honour water rights and bribing public officials.

Murphy wants Chisum's ranch.

Aided by his English neighbour, J. H. Tunstall (Patric Knowles) and young William Bonney, known as Billy The Kid (Geoffrey Deuel), Chisum sets out after the rustlers. In the meantime Sallie arrives together with Murphy's lawyer McSween (Andrew Prine) and his wife Sue (Lynda Day). At a party Sallie is attracted to Billy which disturbs Chisum.

Pat Garrett (Glenn Corbett) a stranger in town rides in to warn Chisum that some Mexican pistoleros are going to rustle his cattle. A fierce gun battle ensues and one of the bandits is captured, but he later "escapes" from the jail of corrupt Sheriff Brady (Bruce Cabot). Realising that Murphy is dishonest, McSween joins up with Chisum.

Chisum and Tunstall decide to open their own general store, to block Murphy, and they send Billy The Kid to Santa Fe for supplies. But the Kid is wounded in an attack on the wagon train by the pistoleros led by Jess Evans (Richard Jaeckel). The Kid is rescued by Garrett and nursed back to

SUM his 201st. FILM

The end of a gun battle with Garrett (Glenn Corbett), Chisum, and Pepper (Ben Johnson) standing over the corpse of their friend McSween (Andrew Prine)

health by Sallie.

Tunstall has decided to inform the Governor (Alan Baxter) of Murphy's evil schemes, but on his way he is killed by two of Sheriff Brady's men, which prompts the Kid to take vengeance into his own hands.

However, Murphy has convinced the Governor that Tunstall was in fact a cattle thief and that his killing had been justified.

The two deputies are captured by Chisum. Garrett and the Kid take them back for trial, but the Kid, after slugging Garrett murders the two men and Brady, before he escapes into the hills. Murphy has persuaded the Governor to appoint a bounty hunter Dan Nodeen (Chris George), as the new Sheriff.

Sallie, now realising the Kid is a born killer, turns to Garrett. The Kid forms his own gang which plans to blow up Murphy's bank. While stealing their way into the general store for dynamite they find McSween and Sue there. Nodeen discovers them and a battle breaks out. Sue leaves the building and rides for Chisum's help. Chisum rounds up his men and rides to town. Coming out of the building to talk to Murphy, McSween is gunned down by Nodeen, and Murphy sets fire to the building to drive out the Kid and his followers. Chisum and his men stampede cattle through the burning town. He then pursues Murphy and kills him. The Kid meanwhile kills Evans, the leader of the pistoleros.

The battle is over, but the Kid, despite the pleas of Garrett who is now the new sheriff, leaves to trail and kill Nodeen. Billy The Kid has become an outlaw while Chisum looks over his domain, once again reassured that peace and order have been restored. . . .

The movie was filmed entirely on location at Durango in Mexico and was directed by Andrew V. McLaglen, with Michael A. Wayne as the Executive Producer. Chisum's ranch was set at the big Marley ranch about thirty-five miles from Durango, while a special Western town was re-created at the village of Chupaderos where most of the existing buildings were given a "new" look.

Chisum is an explosive Western dominated, of course, by the invincible, incredible John "Duke" Wayne, now an Oscar winner through his role in *True Grit*.

KEN JOHNS

1 She is Italian, born with the name Scicolini. Came into films as an extra. Now a superstar, wife of a movie producer, mother of a son.

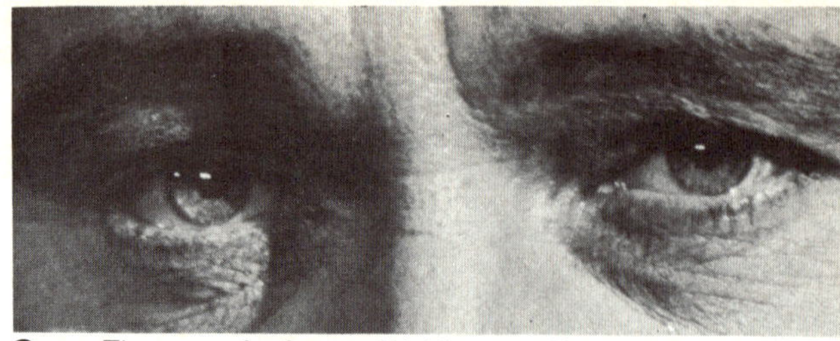

2 The eyes of a famous Welsh actor. His real name is Richard Jenkins. He made his film debut in 1948.

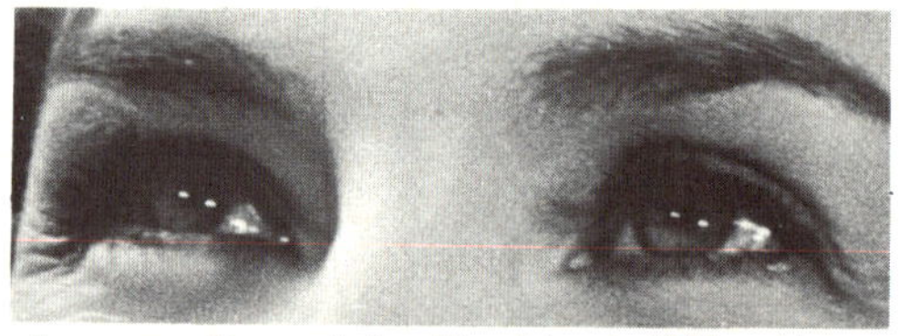

4 She made her film debut in 1955 and is one of the screen's finest actresses.

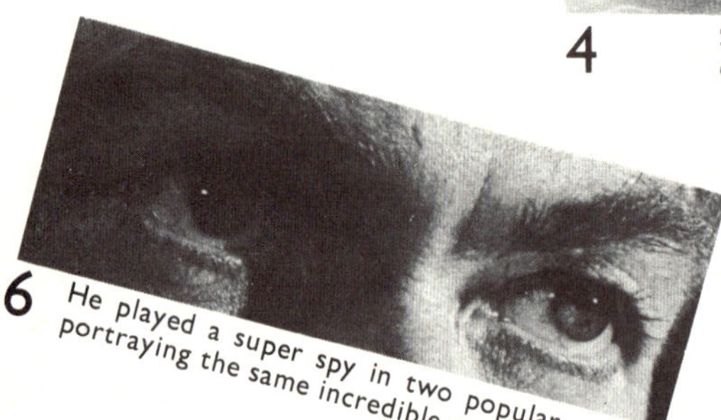

6 He played a super spy in two popular movies portraying the same incredible agent.

7 After starring for many years in a TV Western series he finally got his film breaks in Italy where he quickly gained fame in a violent role.

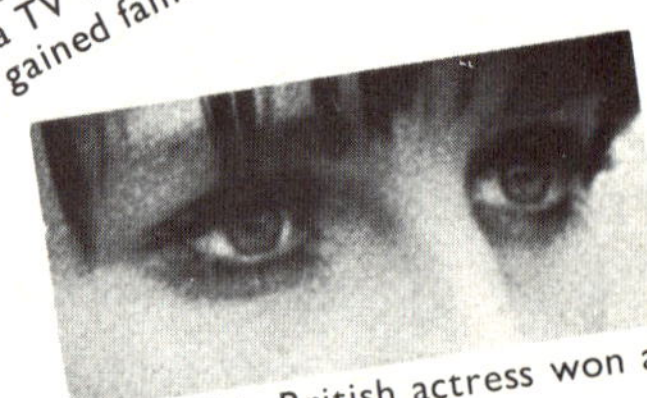

8 This British actress won an Academy Award.

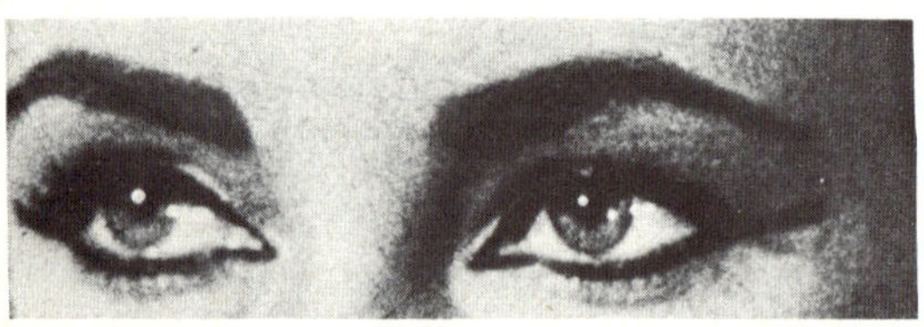

10 Her eyes are perhaps the most famous in movies. She was born in England.

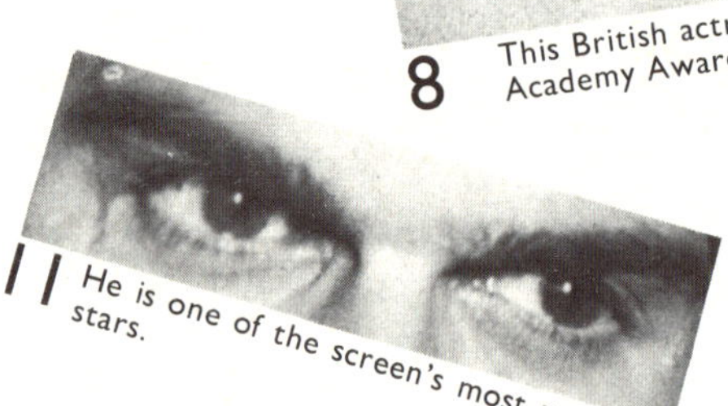

11 He is one of the screen's most romantic stars.

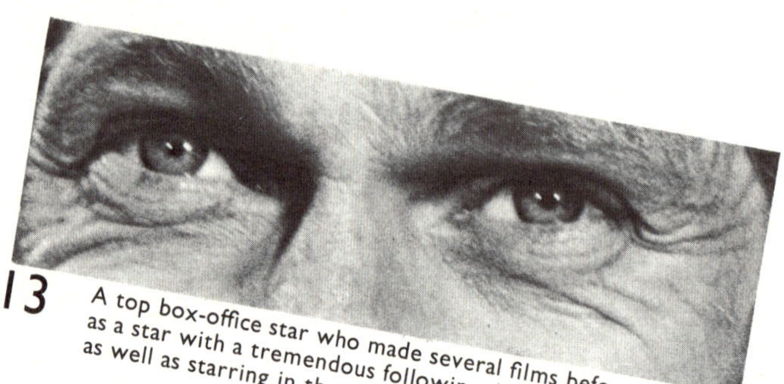

13 A top box-office star who made several films before emerging as a star with a tremendous following. He now produces films as well as starring in them.

14 She is an incredible entertainer with fantastic appeal who won an Oscar in her first film role. Before this she was a successful stage star.

WHOSE EYES?

Can you identify these top stars?

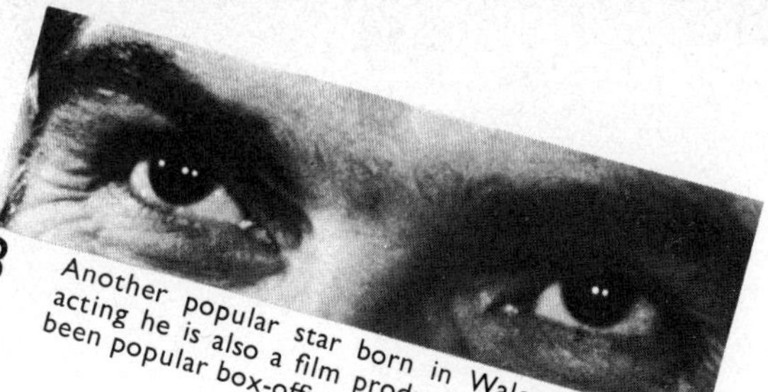

3 Another popular star born in Wales. As well as acting he is also a film producer whose films have been popular box-office successes.

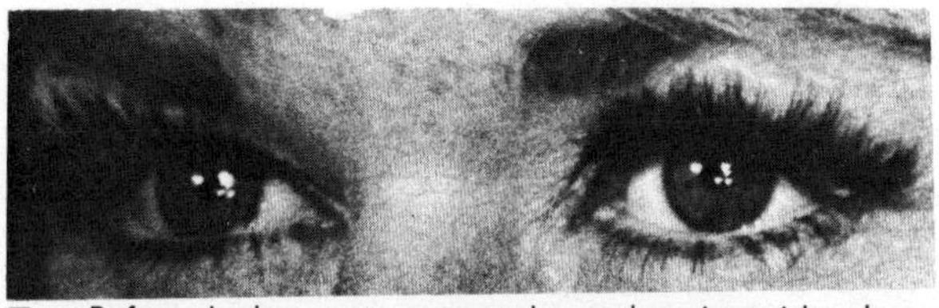

5 Before she became a top star she used to sing with a dance band. Her first film, made in 1948, made her a star overnight.

9 He has a reputation for being a "hell raiser". He has also found fame as a singer.

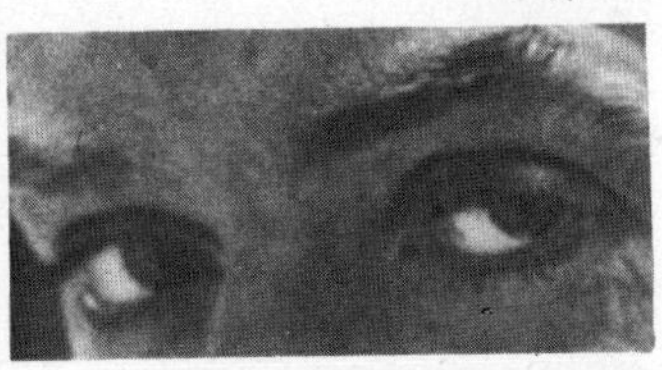

12 First came to fame as an English officer in a spectacular epic film

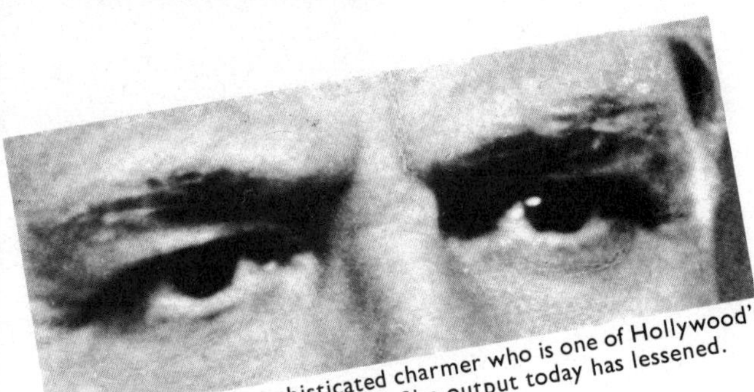

15 The eyes of a sophisticated charmer who is one of Hollywood's greatest stars although his film output today has lessened.

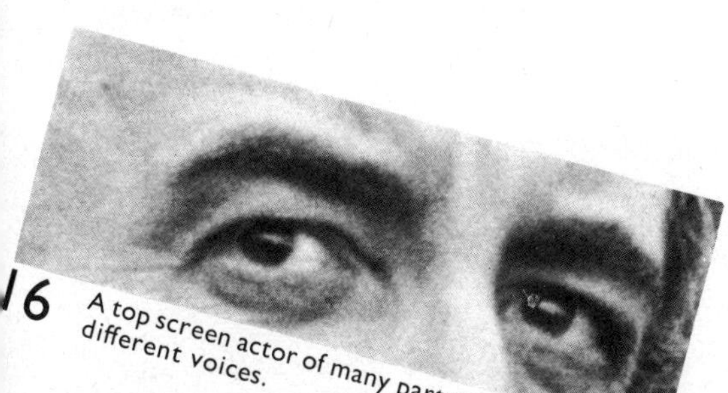

16 A top screen actor of many parts and many different voices.

Answers to Musical Quiz

1. Jeanette Macdonald and Nelson Eddy starred in: *Naughty Marietta* (1934), *Rose Marie* (1935), *Maytime* (1937), *The Girl Of The Golden West* (1938), *Sweethearts* (1939), *New Moon* (1940), *Bitter Sweet* (1940) and *I Married An Angel* (1942).

2. *My Fair Lady* was based on the play "Pygmalion", by George Bernard Shaw.

3. Mitzi Gaynor, seen in *South Pacific*.

4. *Anna And The King Of Siam*, starring Irene Dunne and Rex Harrison.

5. Frank Sinatra, Jules Munshin and Gene Kelly in *On The Town*.

6. Mario Lanza in *The Great Caruso*.

7. Marlon Brando and Jean Simmons sang and danced in *Guys And Dolls*.

8. This famous dancing pair is, of course, Ginger Rogers and Fred Astaire and they appeared together in *Flying Down To Rio* (1933), *The Gay Divorcee* (1934), *Roberta* (1934), *Top Hat* (1935), *Follow The Fleet* (1936), *Swing Time* (1936), *Shall We Dance?* (1937), *Carefree* (1938), *The Story Of Vernon And Irene Castle* (1939) and The Barkleys Of Broadway (1949).

9. *Annie Get Your Gun*. "There's No Business Like Show Business."

10. *The Sound Of Music*.

11. Leonard Bernstein. *West Side Story*.

12. Jean Hagen.

13. Dick Van Dyke. The scene is from *Mary Poppins* and he has also appeared in the musicals *Bye, Bye, Birdie* and *Chitty Chitty Bang Bang*.

14. *Seven Brides For Seven Brothers*.

Answers to 'Whose Eyes?'

1. SOPHIA LOREN
2. RICHARD BURTON
3. STANLEY BAKER
4. JOANNE WOODWARD
5. DORIS DAY
6. JAMES COBURN
7. CLINT EASTWOOD
8. JULIE CHRISTIE
9. RICHARD HARRIS
10. ELIZABETH TAYLOR
11. OMAR SHARIF
12. MICHAEL CAINE
13. STEVE McQUEEN
14. BARBRA STREISAND
15. CARY GRANT
16. PETER SELLERS

Cat Ballou won him an Oscar

As Ben Runsom in Paint Your Wagon

Marvin in action for The Dirty Dozen

ABOVE: Lee with Sharon Acker in Point Blank *one of his most violent films*

TOP: He can look very elegant when he wants to

RIGHT: Toshiro Mifune and Marvin made a strange twosome in Hell In The Pacific, *another tough Marvin movie*

Did you know, that Lee Marvin ...

In his latest film, Monte Walsh*, he and Jack Palance play tough, rough-riding cowboys*

Marvin, as he appeared in Ship Of Fools

Was born in New York on 9th February 1924, the son of Lamont W. Marvin, an advertising executive, and Courtenay Marvin, a leading fashion journalist. The first Marvin was Matthew, who left England to go to America in 1634, and became the first Chief Justice of the State of Connecticut. Another of his ancestors, Ross G. Marvin, was an assistant to Admiral Peary on two of his polar expeditions. He died on the second trip in 1909.

... *Made* his stage debut in a play entitled "Roadside", off Broadway. The play was not particularly successful, but Marvin was noticed. He made his Broadway debut with "Billy Budd". "The opening night was the greatest disappointment of my life. I expected sky rockets and thunder and lightning. Instead, all it was was an opening night. It wasn't at all like I thought it would be," he says reminiscently.

... *Doesn't* think he deserved his Oscar for *Cat Ballou.* "It was just one of those quirks that happened . . . a combination of skill and luck."

. . . *Is* an ex-marine. He was wounded in action in the Pacific campaign in 1944. "I didn't think I'd get out alive," he said with a shudder. But luck was with him, for when he fell wounded, another soldier who had been killed fell on top of him, protecting his body from the shelling. "I tell everyone I was shot in the spine, but in fact I couldn't sit down for weeks!" He still receives a monthly cheque from the Marines in compensation for his injuries.

. . . *Made* his film debut in *You're In The Navy Now* in 1951. The stars were Gary Cooper and Jane Greer. Lee always claims to learn a lot from everyone he works with, and he watches their technique. "I don't think an actor can give a believable performance unless he actually listens to his fellow actors delivering their dialogue."

... *Is* six foot three with green eyes. His hair is white. His eyebrows are dark. He prefers to spend his time either alone, or with a few close friends, away from the bright lights. He is a moody person, one day up, the next right down. "Isn't that what makes an actor . . . or a manic depressive?" he asks wryly. "Turning his emotions on and off?"

. . . *Was* a messenger for a Wall Street company soon after leaving schooldays behind. He laughs as he remembers his experiences there, short-lived though they were. "I went out and bought a fishing rod with my first week's pay. I went fishing at the weekend, broke my hand and got fired. That's when I decided to become an actor."

. . . *Tries* to make all his tough performances look as realistic as possible. "I once had to go to San Quentin prison to do a television show. The prisoners and I hit it off right away. One of them told me that he didn't think of me as an actor but as one of *them.* It was a compliment . . . I think."

. . . *Considers* himself to be independent. "I think independence is something you don't really know. You like to feel independent . . . I think it's a matter of how much you lie to yourself."

. . . *Loves* his work. "I guess you could say that, whatever I'm doing I have fun. I'm just doing what comes naturally."

GREG DAVIS

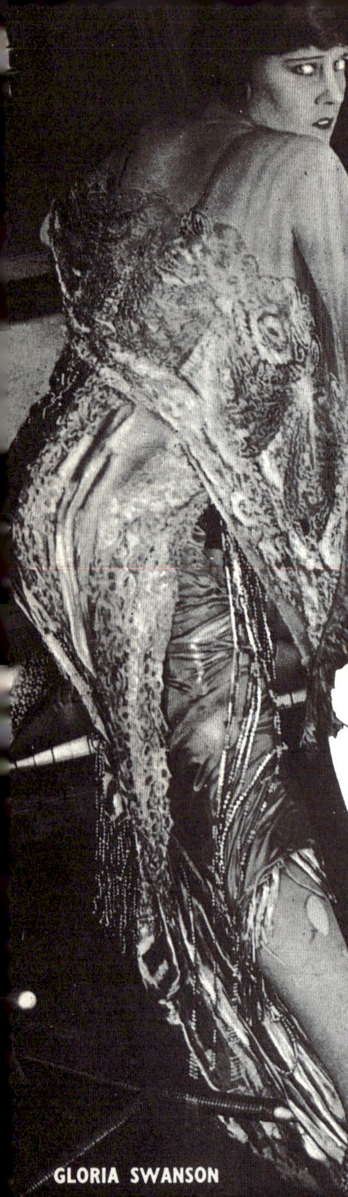

GLORIA SWANSON

THE CHANGING IMAGE OF MOVIE GLAMOUR

Over the years we've seen many changes in the images of the screen's love goddesses. Leslie Wilkinson brings back memories of their Golden Years

BRIGITTE BARDOT

JAYNE MANSFIELD

URSULA ANDRESS

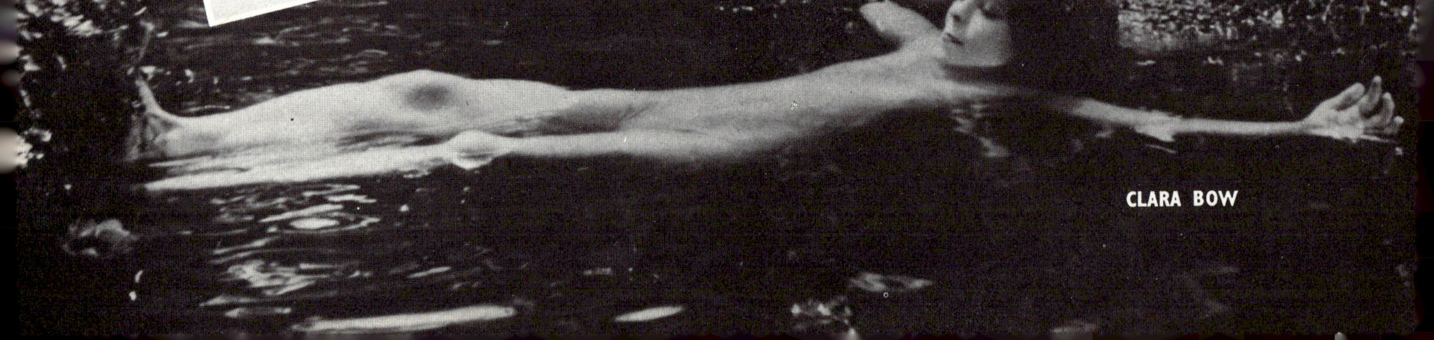

CLARA BOW

DOROTHY LAMOUR

GRETA GARBO

MARILYN MONROE

MARLENE DIETRICH

BETTY GRABLE

● Beauty, it is said, is in the eye of the beholder . . . and so is glamour. What is one man's glamorous meat (or should we call it cheese-cake?) is another's box-office poison.

"Glamour," says the dictionary, "is a charm on the eyes, making them see things as fairer than they really are."

Well, that seems to explain it all . . . and seems to suggest, too, that if we were to meet our glammiest of glamour gals sans hair-do, sans eyelashes, sans make-up, sans what-have-you or what-haven't-you, she would be practically unrecognisable.

Still, that is not the way we meet them on the cinema screen and there must . . . but must . . . be such a thing as natural glamour.

In Edwardian days it was the "thing" for pretty stage actresses to be portrayed on picture postcards for sale in newsagents and at railway station bookstalls . . . and one of the most beautiful and definitely the best-seller among these was Gladys Cooper, who is still with us and whose beauty and acting ability still adorns the stage and the occasional film (remember her as one of the aunts in *A Nice Girl Like Me?*).

But with the advent of films their own individual styles of glamour came into being and very varied these styles have been. The overall accent, however, seems always to have been for something larger than life . . . and although the ladies concerned (we are only dealing with ladies here, despite the fact that there *are* glamour boys, too) were often shy and home-loving girls, their studios' publicity could build them up into the sexiest of sex symbols.

One of the earliest and most notorious of these publicity build-ups was that for Theodosia Goodman, a tailor's daughter from Cincinnati, who was moulded into the famous screen siren, Theda Bara. This name is an anagram on "Death Arab" and as it was thought that an Arabian woman would be a welcome and novel addition to the screen, a fantastic story was woven regarding Theda's birth in the shadow of the Pyramids, the child of a sheik and an Egyptian princess. Theda was, of course, the original screen vampire and made a number of successful silent films, including her own interpretations of Camille, Dubarry, Cleopatra and Salome. She figured on picture postcards of the period, as did Pearl White, the Serial Queen.

This was also the era of the Mack Sennett Bathing Beauties, whose dash to the beach provided many a finale to

(continued overleaf)

(continued)

these hilarious silent comedies. Most of the Beauties became stars of big feature productions, prominent among them being Marie Prevost, Phyllis Haver and Gloria Swanson.

The 1920's ushered in a whole series of glamour queens.

Early on we had the elegant Betty Blythe, remembered chiefly for *The Queen Of Sheba* (1921) and *Chu Chin Chow* (1923), the exotic Nazimova, the overpowering Nita Naldi (real name Anita Dooley), Gloria Swanson and Pola Negri.

The later 1920's produced less overpowering glamour stars, such as Colleen Moore, "the girl with the boyish bob" and star of *Flaming Youth* . . . and Vilma Banky, the blonde Austrian lovely who was the heroine of Valentino's last film, *Son Of The Sheik* (1925).

And then in 1927 came the "It" girl – Clara Bow, so named from this definition of sex appeal by the "daring" romantic novelist, Elinor Glyn.

The "blonde bombshell" Jean Harlow, whose platinum-blonde loveliness more than decorated *Hell's Angels* (1930), *Red Dust* (1932) and *Reckless* (1934), among other films, became the new rage in the 1930's.

The 1930's was also the film heyday of Mae West, who triumphed from 1932 onwards (in *Night After Night, She Done Him Wrong* and *I'm No Angel*). Another household word for glamour was Hedy Lamarr. After the much-publicised nude sequence in *Ecstasy* (1933), her beauty and acting ability were used to great effect in *Algiers* (1938) and *Lady Of The Tropics* (1939). Her career extended successfully through the 1940's . . . and another star who shone glamorously through the same two decades was Dorothy Lamour.

Her first film was *The Jungle Princess* (1936), after which she became typecast as "the sarong girl". Films such as *Hurricane* (1937), *Typhoon* (1940), *Aloma Of The South Seas* (1941) naturally necessitated this, but "Dottie" Lamour was also an accomplished comedienne, as witness her co-starring with Bing Crosby and Bob Hope in the *Road* pictures.

Glamour in the mid-1930's suffered something of a setback as feminine film fans began to show a preference for stars with whom they could identify themselves, more homely people such as Carole Lombard, Claudette Colbert and Norma Shearer, rather than the more goddess-like types. Included with these could be Lana Turner, who in her earliest films such as *Love Finds Andy Hardy* and *Calling Doctor Kildare* (both in 1939) was the perfect example of "the girl next door".

Betty Grable was also making her first impact round about this time, but it was during the war years that both Lana and Betty became two of the forces' favourite pin-ups: Betty, "the girl with the million-dollar legs" and Lana, "the sweater girl" ("I like to pull their eyes over the wool").

Alongside them at the top were Rita Hayworth, "the strawberry blonde", who dazzled in *Blood And Sand* (1941), *Cover Girl* (1942), *Gilda* (1946), *Lady From Shanghai* (1947) – and Jane Russell, "mean, moody and magnificent", who burst on to a delighted masculine world in *The Outlaw* (1943), which film, however, was held up for three years by censor trouble and the publicity campaign which emphasised Miss Russell's physical attributes.

Also prominent in the 1940's was the lovely Ann Sheridan, "the oomph girl" . . . and the highly decorative Virginia Mayo and Veronica Lake, "the peek-a-boo bang" girl.

It should be remembered that these ladies were far more than just pretty faces, and throughout the 1950's and 1960's were giving sterling performances in a variety of films.

The 1950's produced that star who has been called "the pin-up girl supreme": Marilyn Monroe. She adorned over twenty films in the decade before her tragic and untimely death in 1962, when she was mourned by filmgoers everywhere.

Gina Lollobrigida and Brigitte Bardot ("the sex kitten") have survived almost two decades as glamour goddesses and the statuesque Anita Ekberg will be remembered when the majority of her films will have been forgotten.

Ava Gardner should, of course, be mentioned, having once been voted "the world's most beautiful woman" and Marlene Dietrich has continued to exercise a glamorous spell from the days of *The Blue Angel* (1930).

Elizabeth Taylor has shone for years in the glamour of a well-publicised private life, but has emerged from it all during the last decade as one of the screen's finest actresses.

In the glamour stakes of the 1960's, only Ursula Andress and Raquel Welch appear to have been outstanding from among the new entrants . . . and now, what are the prospects of the 1970's?

Well, there's Raquel Welch in *Myra Breckinridge* . . . and what's this? She's co-starring with Mae West!

Why, that's almost where we came in!

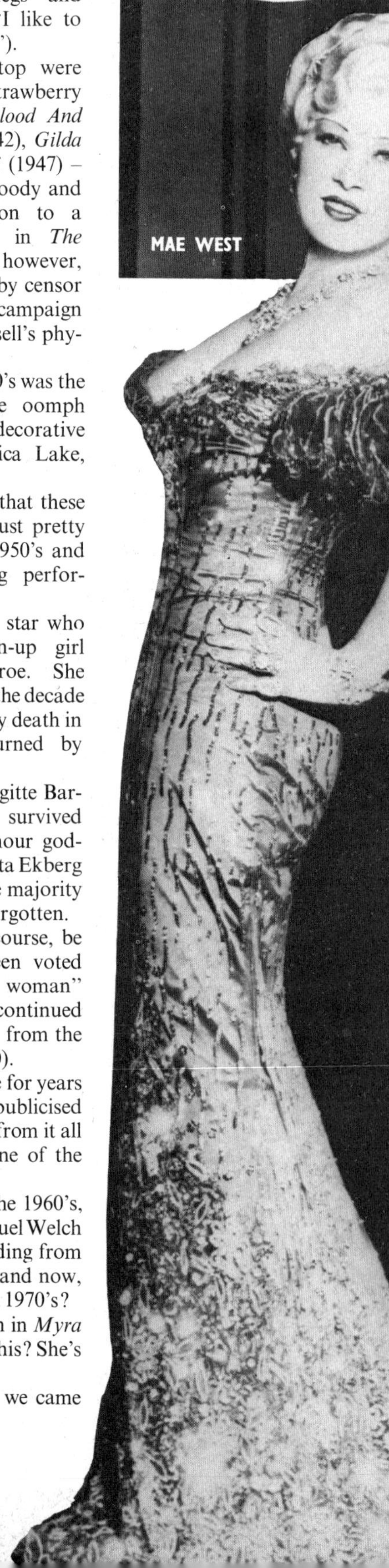

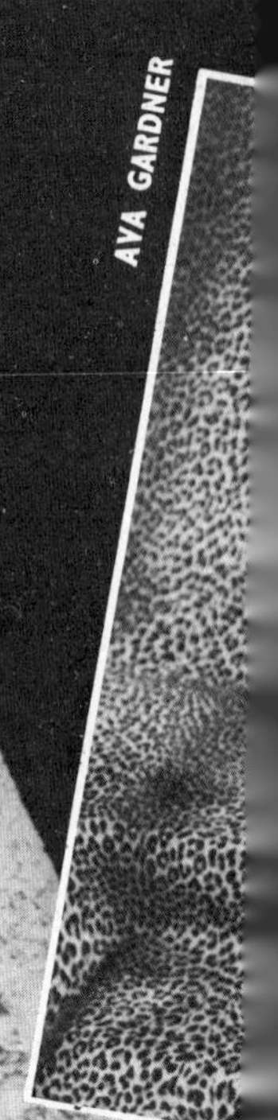